J V D

Educationists
and Their Vanities:
One Hundred Missives
to My Colleagues

George F. Kneller

D0111640

i

Educationists and Their Vanities:
One Hundred Missives to My Colleagues

By George F. Kneller

Copyright 1994 by George F. Kneller

Published by Caddo Gap Press
3145 Geary Boulevard, Suite 275
San Francisco, California 94118

Overseas representative:
Drake Publishing Services Limited
St. Fagans Road, Fairwater, Cardiff CF5 3AE
United Kingdom

Published in cooperation with the
Council of Learned Societies in Education

List Price - $15.95

ISBN 1-880192-12-8

Library of Congress Cataloging-in-Publication Data

Kneller, George F. (George Frederick), 1908-
    Educationists and their vanities : one hundred missives to my
colleagues / George F. Kneller.
        p.   cm.
    ISBN 1-880192-12-8 : $15.95
    1. Teacher educators--United States. 2. Education--Study and
teaching (Higher)--United States. 3. Education--United States-
-Graduate work. 4. Education--United States--Philosophy.
5. Education--Research--United States.   I. Title.
LB1737.5.U5K64   1994
370'.7'30973--dc20   94-27894
                                                              CIP

Table of Contents

For My Brother Jack.

"Everything's been said already, but as no one listens, we must always begin again."
—André Gide

Foreword

Professor George F. Kneller was a participant in and keen observer of the activities and development of the School of Education (ultimately to become the Graduate School of Education) of the University of California, Los Angeles, over a period of several decades. During this time, UCLA grew with the city of Los Angeles to rank with the Berkeley campus as one of the major centers of scholarship in the United States and, indeed, the world. And, during this time, the School evolved from a primary emphasis on teaching and teacher education to primary occupation with research. This has been the story of many sister institutions of higher education over the second half of the twentieth century.

From the time of his coming to UCLA in 1953 and on into retirement, Professor Kneller has been a keenly-observant critic, often vocal in regard to both shifts in emphasis and the preoccupations of colleagues. Few escaped his sharp words entirely; many were the focal point of his criticisms. He has very little use for the methods of a great deal of the so-called research he decries and less for its potential use in the world of educational affairs. He amuses some of his colleagues, raises the blood pressure of others, but has never been ignored; there usually is a nervousness to the laughter he induces.

One of the problems of academe is the difficulty of securing tangible feedback regarding the significance of what one does. There is not the highly visible evidence of a bridge or house one helped to build. Work receiving widespread public acclaim frequently is frowned upon by colleagues. And colleagues often are the last to comment on the book just published or the special award just announced. Given these circumstances, it is exceedingly helpful to have hard-nosed colleagues who, rightly or wrongly, subject what you are doing to sharp criticism. This tends to promote introspection, and candid introspection is something all of us need to cultivate. In this regard, George Kneller serves us well.

—John I Goodlad
Professor and Director
Center for Educational Renewal
University of Washington

Preface

began writing these *Missives* in 1957 to expose what I considered were radical flaws in the study of education and the training of teachers. I am publishing them now because the flaws are still there. I want to relay my message not only to schools of education but to all people seriously concerned by the immense problems facing education today, problems for which, in my view, our schools of education are in good measure responsible.

The *Missives* appear in their original order because they deal with issues and events that occurred at the time they were written. They embrace a range of themes, *e.g.*, the art of teaching, the human sciences, multiculturalism, egalitarianism, postmodernism, and, above all, the study of education itself.

Throughout, I recall the university to its true mission—to seek knowledge and pass it on, to teach as well as to research, each process stimulating the other. In this quest I advocate a balanced, discipline-based undergraduate education as against the mix of fashionable electives offered on most campuses. If my ideal sounds autocratic and restrictive, that is only by comparison with today's excessive permissivism. In reality it is the only coherent, intellectually sound option we have, and I defend it against the trendy topics inundating today's curricula.

xi

Too many of these topics replace reason, objectivity, and science with extreme relativism, racial and ethnic separatism, and the facile belief that "anything goes." Often reducing knowledge to minority perspectives, their aim is not truth so much as empowerment. Regrettably, many faculty ignore this assault on the mind, preferring to bury themselves in innocuous, marginal research.

In these *Missives* I especially indict schools of education, which use their lock on teacher training to promote naive reforms of little or no demonstrated value to public education. These reforms betray a prevailing corruption in the study of education itself. Instead of building a genuine discipline, educationists pursue research programs too many of which are intellectually sterile. They model their studies chiefly on psychology and sociology, which are zoos of conflicting theories, with no sound evidence to choose among them. Educational psychology especially has perpetrated thousands of futile microstudies of processes like teaching and learning, ignoring the fact that they are too complex and variable to be accurately measured.

Education faculties boast of being practical, yet instead of refining the art of teaching, they spend millions trying to prove it's a technology based on science. Instead of exemplifying the art, they disseminate questionable techniques. No wonder so many of our young teachers are unprepared to teach. No wonder so many of our kids don't learn.

These *Missives* deal not only with prevailing weaknesses in schools of education, they suggest ways they can be eliminated. Basic to all these ways is reform in the study and teaching of education itself. To effect this, we must draw mainly on history, philosophy, and literature, along with cultural anthropology, the least doctrinaire of the human sciences. As the *Missives* clearly state, there is no scientific explanation of education. Neither psychology, nor sociology, nor biology will do the job. Instead we must use the tools of interpretation that have long served the student of human nature in its cultural context. These belong mainly to literary appreciation, philosophic analysis, historical understanding, and participant observation.

Though a newcomer, the discipline of education, once developed, would crown the humanities in virtue of the range of its subject matter and its twofold character, both theoretical and practical. The discipline could be studied both for its own sake and as an entree to a career. In its practical capacity it would supply examples of the arts of teaching and administering from history, literature, and anthropology, examples more deeply felt, more dramatic, more personal, more persuasive than generalizations from psychology and sociology. In this capacity, too, it would offer reflections of philosophers, the most rigorous of thinkers, on the manifold problems of education. These reflections may shun details but they go to the heart of the matter. They provide lessons that are broader, more enduring, more fundamental to the techniques we so uncritically purvey. If the study of education is derided by colleagues in other fields, we educationists have ourselves to blame. Until our research is founded on more substantive, more firmly organized knowledge, most of it will remain of little use. Until our pedagogy is grounded in this knowledge, courses in methods of teaching will continue to be of little practical value.

In these *Missives* I use and quote many authors without footnoting their work. This is because I am writing a personal, not an academic, book. The *Missives* have been called an intellectual biography, a unique, succinct record of one man's thinking on educational problems of many kinds. Admittedly unconventional, this book invites readers to think unconventionally.

Through the years I've learned much from my students and colleagues, and most of it remains inseparable from my thought. Their observations made me revise many of my ideas, while dooming others. I'm indeed grateful for this and other valuable help. Without it my product would have been much the poorer.

—George F. Kneller

1

Where Are We Headed?

joined this School of Education four years ago, and there is nowhere I'd rather teach. Yet I am disturbed by the School's attitude to its functions and its relations with the University. There is a yawning gap between promise and performance. For four years there has been talk of reform, yet I see none. Talk, too, of basing educational policies on substantive knowledge. No sign of that, either. We now have a "Ten–Year Program" that barely updates the agenda of 1953. Are we serious about reform?

Last April President Sproul hosted an all-campus conference at Asilomar to discuss the University of California's role in state and national higher education. The conference adopted some historic resolutions, four of which are crucial for this School and its Ten-Year Program. I will cite them in order and highlight their significance, not just for us but for schools of education everywhere:

◆ The University's first function is to "promote research that advances our understanding of the natural world and interprets the great creations of human insight and imagination." In this School how much research and teaching will interpret these works? What content is involved?

◆ The University's second function is to teach "not merely by

1

transmitting established knowledge and skills but also by helping students experience the actual processes of testing new hypotheses and producing fresh interpretations." How will our faculty meet this challenge? Will our teachers outperform others, as they should? Will we break the habits that negate our ideals?

◆ The University's third function is to train the young for professional careers—"a training grounded in the relevant sciences and literatures...and enlightened by methods that expand the boundaries of knowledge." Will this school adopt this approach? Will we teach methods that promote discovery, or will we pass on the old rules of thumb, tricks of the trade for the unimaginative? Will we carry out a program fit for a great University or cling to practices that differ little from those of state colleges, business schools, and think tanks?

◆ The University's fourth function is to perform public services that are "germane to its mission, support other functions, and are superior to the services of other institutions." In other words, will our school surveys and advisory missions contribute only to the agency served or, additionally, to the understanding of education as such? Will this School finally shed the provincialism typical of a local college?

September 1957

2

The Next Ten Years

The Asilomar Conference decided that the state colleges, not the University, should prepare elementary and secondary school teachers. With teachers in short supply, however, no action was taken on this decision. So, over the next decade, should we spend more time on training teachers or less? I recommend a fifth year devoted to the preparation of teachers.

In the next ten years we shall have to decide on the proper nature of our work. The study of education is both academic and professional. As an academic study, education is a humanity, not a science, although it includes some elements from the human or social sciences. As a professional study, education draws on public administration, politics, law, and finance. In its practical phases, it is more appropriate to speak of "schooling."

We educationists not only should lecture on successful teaching but practice it. We should combine the top-down approach so convenient to the lecturer with a bottom-up approach that encourages student initiative and self-expression. We dilate on concepts like broad fields, correlation, core, and integration, yet how many of us put any of them into practice? Do we really teach differently at the graduate level? Do we change our content?

Take doctoral dissertations. Who reads them? Overspecialized, overestimated, and overweight, they represent the triumph of pedantry over intellect in ever-diminishing fields with ever-dwindling applications. I have been too often lost in these saharas of the spirit. The dissertation once was expected to make a contribution to knowledge. Let's restore that ideal. If you and your students can't contribute, don't try. From now on let every dissertation be written with the intent to publish. Let it be an enduring monograph, not more paper for the stacks.

Without agreement on principles there can be none on policy, much less practice. I find it deplorable that in schools of education at top universities so many faculty should think so little of theory or principle. Unfortunately, this intolerance of theory, this refusal to agree on central purposes, has allowed practices to flourish that are an affront to great universities.

Instead of giving the old structure another paint job, let's probe this School's foundations. How firm are they? In the next ten years we must agree on basic educational principles. We must concur on the central mission of the School within this University and within academia generally. In future *Missives* I shall spell out what I believe that mission should be.

September 1957

3

Our Place in a University

It has been proposed that we work out our views of the School's mission in a public forum, at which interested lay persons would contribute their own views. This is a bad idea. A public forum might yield a couple of original ideas, but it also would produce a gridlock of conflicting opinions. We already have been surfeited with advice from outside, very little of it the product of deep thought, not enough of it specific to the work of this School.

I do not wish to devalue public opinion, for we must respond to the culture(s) beyond our walls. Our mission obviously includes public service, but faculty who trim their views to primarily public problems will find that the University stands for nothing but what the public dictates. It will become just another social institution, shorn of its originality, bereft of its special purpose, standing for anything...and everything.

It also has been suggested that we invite experts to advise us how to proceed. Another bad idea. I don't decry experts as such, we might get an idea or two from them. But we are supposed to be experts, and there must be few good ideas for this School that would not occur to at least one of us. Let's respect our own abilities!

However, we should take the advice of our students. Here is some of what I have heard:

◆ Undefined Goals: Some courses have hazy objectives. Some require students to memorize masses of facts and regurgitate them on exams—facts rarely discussed in class or related to current problems. Controversy is avoided. Professors don't like you to argue.

◆ Personalities on Parade: In some classes instructors dilate on their private lives. No matter what problem comes up, it recalls something in their experience. How much do students generalize from a professor's anecdotes? Do they become clones of their teachers?

◆ Papers and Exams: Papers, if returned at all, lack constructive comments. Exams are used as measures of achievement, not as teaching devices. Blue books rarely are annotated. How can students correct their mistakes if they are not identified?

All of us know that schools of education rank low on the academic totem. We should strive all the more to raise the standards of our discipline.To this end we should seek the advice of colleagues throughout the campus. At the same time we should offer our solutions to problems throughout the University of California system. After all, in education we are the professionals and we should never sell ourselves short.

October 1957

6

4

Education: "Marketplace of Ideas"

The metaphor is apt. In education more ideas are produced and distributed than in any other area of study. Whether the marketplace and the ideas are orderly is another matter. How can we make education a well-ordered marketplace of well-conceived ideas?

I take my text from Alfred North Whitehead: "We are only just now realizing that education requires a genius and study of its own." Without this insight education is hardly an interesting subject. Unless we define and order our subject matter, education will remain the outsider among established disciplines.

What is a discipline? It is an intellectual enterprise with a domain of study, a body of data, concepts, and theories, and a set of techniques for gaining, validating, and applying knowledge. Education is all this and more. It is a field of study with the knowledge to guide intellectual, moral, and emotional development.

We must determine the nature and structure of this knowledge. How does it relate to and compare with knowledge in other disciplines? These issues have not seriously been discussed. It seems to be assumed that educational practices are justified by experience alone. If they "work," that's all we need, though the meaning of "work" is rarely analyzed. To work properly, these practices must be based on principles refined by

7

the study of education as an academic discipline.

Some critics deny that education ever can be a discipline. Its subject matter is too varied, they say, and is not organized logically or hierarchically by theories and concepts native to education. This criticism assumes that a discipline must be modeled on mathematics or the natural sciences. But many disciplines are not organized logically at all. English, for instance, encompasses language, literature, composition, speech, and communication. Does anyone doubt that English is a discipline?

It's unfortunate that much of this deflationary work is done by educationists themselves. For the foreseeable future the main task of schools of education should be to enhance the study of Education as a genuine university discipline, no less, and in some ways more, deserving than other disciplines in the curriculum.

November 1957

5

The Traitor Within

hese *Missives* have found their mark! All full professors in the School of Education met secretly. The agenda? How to handle the traitor within. The discussion was not *ad argumentum*, as it should have been, but *ad hominem*. The critic had to be silenced. But how? After all, I had tenure, had done nothing immoral, and certainly was not incompetent. After some wrangling, it was decided to (a) send me to Coventry, (b) keep the meeting secret, (c) ask the Dean to find me a job elsewhere, (d) meet again to decide what else to do.

At the second meeting only three or four professors showed up, so no further action was taken.

Not being in on the plot, imagine my surprise when I greeted full professors with my usual hello and got no reply. I was being snubbed! Ostracized! Since assistant professors were as friendly as ever, I began to suspect what was up. The silent treatment did not trouble me at all. I thought it was pathetic.

After a couple of weeks a repentant colleague came to my office to reveal the plot and apologize. He had vowed secrecy only to please his colleagues, but in all decency he could not keep up the charade. Others followed. All expressed regret. The Dean seems in no hurry to find me another job; in fact he has recommended a promotion, while urging me to be more

9

considerate.

So the campaign collapsed. One of the ringleaders had me to lunch and gave me fatherly advice on how to get along with my colleagues. Another asked me to help him plan a doctoral program for school administrators, all of whom would take my philosophy course. A third wanted me to lecture his class on the meaning of meaning—which I did.

But I have made a momentous decision. To prevent more paranoia, I will set these *Missives* aside. If I resume, I will take a lighter, more humorous tack. My message, however, will not be diluted. **Irony** and **satire** will replace up–front castigation. I conclude with apologies to Lord Byron:

> *Thus **irony**, deep and slow, exhausting thought,*
> *In meditation dwelt, with learning wrought,*
> *And hiving wisdom with each studious year,*
> *Which stings its foes to wrath, which grows from fear;*
> *And **satire** answers to all doubts so clear.*

December 1957

6

Rural Education: Call to Action!

Ten years after dispatching *Missive 5*, I am drawn back to work by the urgent need to solve our rural education problems as successfully as we solved our urban problems. Just think:

◆ One third of Americans live in rural areas. They form our largest minority and hence present a formidable social problem we teachers of teachers are morally bound to address.

◆ The average rural worker earns 20% less than the average urban worker, thus creating a shameful poverty problem we cannot ignore.

◆ Rural areas have a higher dropout rate than that of any other minority group.

◆ Rural living is hazardous. A hailstorm strikes or a horde of locusts swoops, and in minutes an entire crop is destroyed. Rust and thistle choke the grain. Foxes kill chickens. The resulting deprivation blights the lives of millions of underprivileged Americans.

It also creates an urgent educational problem. We must

11

become more sensitive to, more concerned about, this long-neglected sector of our population. We must act now to:

◆ Spread ruralism, like urbanism, throughout our curriculum, introducing courses in rural education problems, rural history, rural minority culture, and other sorts of ruralisms.

◆ Set up special programs, courses, field trips, and team teaching to help eliminate rural poverty, dropouts, discrimination, and a host of inequities and injustices that our largest minority has suffered since this great country was founded.

◆ Submit major research requests to every available funding agency for at least $10 million to get the job done.

◆ Create special admissions policies, procedures, and privileges to facilitate the required flexibility.

◆ Appoint an Assistant Dean of Rural Problems to organize, supervise, regularize, activate, fulminate, and above all, form a Faculty Committee on Rural Problems.

Colleagues! This is the moment to make our School a real force in the life of the community. To this end I shall leave shortly on a fact-finding trip to all deprived rural areas of the world, for which I naturally have a grant, renewable when further research is needed. On my return I will report my findings and recommend solutions. Meantime, pardon my irony, satire, clichés, and specialist lingo, and just look at the research potential!

September 1967

7

Rural Education: Questions Answered

Back from my world trip of ruralities, I find my colleagues anxious to get going on our Ruralities Program. So let me field a few questions:

◆ **How will rural education problems connect with urban ones?** We must clarify the relationship, using systems analysis and game theory to guarantee outcomes.

◆ **What precisely will the outcomes be?** Precise outcomes depend on precise behavioral objectives.

◆ **What objectives should the faculty propose?** This is a matter for initial exploration, calling for a Committee on Exploration. I suggest visibility as a viable objective.

◆ **What about classes and students?** No need. For the first two years, we shall be fully occupied with exploratory studies and pilot programs. We shall assemble a rich variety of variables, dependent and independent, intervening and extravening, immediate, intermediate, and extramediate, coordinated with multivariant correlates and the latest hardware and software. Such fieldwork guarantees a major breakthrough.

13

◆ **Should we create an Area of Ruralities?** Yes, indeed. It would be chaired by an Assistant Dean of Ruralities and would include senior researchers, junior researchers, research assistants, secretaries, typists, and assorted poobahs. Since we live in a democracy, all would have the vote.

◆ **How should we spend our $10 million grant?** Why not blow it on a retreat? Get away from phones. Cruise the world. Pump in creativity and pump out routine. No need to take action. Just issue a report. Deduct all expenses from income taxes and charge them to the grant. To organize this thing, we need an Assistant Dean of Retreats, with rich experience in retreating.

◆ **What should we do with our philosophers of education?** Pack 'em off on a missing-concepts mission. There is no place in our Program for cognitive dissonance.

◆ **Will our Program succeed?** Absolutely! We are on the cutting edge of knowledge. We are America in motion. Our program will impact.

◆ **And the secret of our success?** Don't mess with reality. Invent it!

September 1968

8

Rural Problems: Advice from Politicos

t is imperative to canvass the major politicos on rural education problems, so that we can vote our conscience on election day. Here is a sample of what they say:

◆ George Wallace: "We're gonna bring law and order to the countryside and keep city slickers and university eggheads away from our farmers' daughters. We're gonna get the Federal government out of rural bedrooms and give them back to the states."

◆ A Distinguished Rural Senator: "My fellow Americans, I am sending a signal to all our rural brothers and sisters that we no longer will tolerate the social discrimination they have suffered since the founding of this great nation. I call on all right-minded Americans to stop calling farmers hicks, yokels, hayseeds, and cornpokes because they chew tobacky and eat pork rinds. America is a moral country, and farmers are our most precious minority. We say, enough is enough. We're not going to take it any more!"

◆ Richard M. Nixon: "I shall have nothing to say on rural problems. I will not be responsible in any way for upsetting the talks now going on in the private sector."

15

◆ **Hubert H. Humphrey**: "Fellow Americans, I promise that if I am elected, I will end all disparities between rural and urban education and all other kinds of education in this wonderful country of ours. I endorse the entire rural Democratic platform and will be ready to debate all sides of the issue."

◆ **George Meany**: "The Union does not advocate any political platform on rural problems except the one it advocates. I quote it to you *verbatim* and wish to commend a certain department at UCLA for being alert to our needs and aware of our special grievances:

> *Schools serving rural poors are in many cases even less able than the inner-city schools to meet the needs of the twentieth century.... Rural and urban problems are interrelated, with today's low-income rural children becoming the poor and unemployed of the cities of tomorrow. Rural education, like urban education, requires massive support from the federal government."*

There you have it, colleagues! In our time peace is war, poverty is wealth, and minorities are majorities; so rural problems are urban problems. However, further research will be needed to dispel the notion that something is not quite right here. We shall have to examine the multifaceted plurisignificance of the rural–urban interface and the all–important research nexus.

Fall 1968

9

Rural Problems: How to Solve Them

 ust received is the following telegram from our good friends, the United States Department of Health, Wealth, and Happiness:

YOUR FUNDS ARE NOW DEPLETED. PLEASE SUBMIT YOUR INITIAL RURALITIES REPORT IMMEDIATELY.

This refers to our grant under PL 47b 542/Oct Section A Subsection c/500 Title IIIa, c, and q.

The Chicken Feed Corporation also has laid it on the line. Either we persuade more chickens to eat their corn or the Corporation will cut off our funds.

We therefore are calling an emergency faculty meeting for this afternoon with the following agenda:

◆ **Planning**: Do we plan for now or for now and then?

◆ **Organization**: Should we organize today or tomorrow? Please be ready with your input.

◆ **Administration**: No organization without administration! Nothing will fly till the faculty members are agreed on the agenda.

◆ **Initial Steps**: Run first, walk later. Do we take the initial steps now or refer them to a committee?

◆ **Facing the Facts**: The future is now. The world is changing rapidly and it is not too early to head into the next century. Megatrends impact us all. Our disinformation age drowns in hype and hogwash, and there is a serious reality gap, which this faculty must fill.

◆ **Decision-Making**: Let's use decision theory. We can assume the majority will prevail, yet minorities must be heard. Since a majority is the sum of its minorities, a majority decision is a collective minority one. Thus all sides win and confrontation is avoided.

◆ **Evaluation**: UCLA's Graduate School of Education leads the world in this crucial field, so let's draw on our unrivaled expertise to solve our problems. After a multi-year, in-depth study of near and far evaluation theories, our R & D Center has concluded that further research is needed, and more support funds are required to sustain continuing cooperative involvement.

Fall 1968

10

"And Gladly Would He Facilitate"

With funds for ruralities depleted, we are ready for our next major breakthrough: LEARNING FACILITATION, a powerful and dramatic innovation in student-teacher relations.

My big Webster gives one meaning for "facilitate," namely "make things easier," and several for "facilitation," one being "the lowering of the threshold for reflex conduction along a particular neural pathway, especially from repeated use of that pathway." (Who else but a psychologist would have written that?)

The Graduate School of Education cannot linger over semantics. We have a job to do. The wheels already are turning, so let's assume that we know the true meaning of facilitation.

The Academic Senate finally has approved a new rank of "learning facilitator" to replace that of instructor. There will be the usual three steps to the rank of assistant professor of learning facilitation.

Course LF 100 also has been approved, but owing to its unique content and method of instruction, no facilitator has been assigned. The course is required of all wannabe LFers.

The Regents, the Legislature, and the Governor all have applauded our LF program and built it into their platforms under "tax savings." (A complete LF operation cuts instructional costs 90 per cent, leaving more funds for urgent building construction.)

Now for the catch. Students who consent to having their learning facilitated insist on being paid for it. Last week they marched on Sacramento with a non-negotiable demand for at least $100 a week for allowing themselves to be LFed. They also have requested private cubicles for LFing.

After much study, our evaluation experts have recommended a program of self-evaluation, but more research is needed.

What next? Our Dean of LFing has applied for a grant to research how to LF without teaching. Meantime, here's to the future of LFing, the GSE's great gift to educators everywhere!

March 1970

11

If It Ain't Broke, Why Fix It?

"So on what does your father do?"

"He works for a reorganization."

The latest "Reorganization Plan" testifies to the delusion that any reform is better than none. The Plan displays some of the worst features of university government today. It assumes, for example, that educational decisions should be made by majority vote in representative bodies, as though the university were a nation or a state. Yet not even congressional committees are created by majority vote. They are appointed. Seniority counts, even in a democracy.

The Plan overwhelms the faculty with administrative chores. The proposed Advisory Committee is loaded with duties that only an oligarchy with a host of secretarial assistants could hope to handle. Professors joining this committee must be prepared to surrender half their productive time. Indeed the Plan is one more assault on a professor's prime duties, which are to teach and research.

No good reason is given for replacing the Peer Review Committee with a Personnel Committee. The latter simply repeats the flaws of its predecessor with flaws of its own. Its "representative patterns" reflect the current craze for egalitarianism at all costs. This committee may have seven members of any single faculty rank. Or it may have five from one rank, who can outvote the other two. Or all ranks may be represented equally. *O Tempora Dementata!*

In this administrative wonderland, entities multiply. In addition to the Personnel Committee, the Advisory Committee, and the Educational Policies Committee, there is an Executive Council, which (since there are six Areas and 20+ Programs) will stagger under 26+ members. What a crazy quilt of authority figures!

The Plan takes aim at leadership, here perceived as "elitist" and therefore ripe for rejection. Since deans and chairmen will each have only one vote, a caucus of assistant professors could undercut them. But without this leadership there is little chance of decisive, creative action. Who will resolve the crises the faculty causes but cannot handle?

The Plan shuffles the shards of previous plans and practices, creating a new combination more cumbersome and demanding than its predecessor. It tinkers with everything in range for reasons having little to do with Education.

Easy, then, colleagues! If it ain't broke, why fix it?

May 1970

12

Consciousness-Raising: Curricular Tours de Force

fter years of intensive study, funded by the Gullible Foundation, our Select Committee on Consciousness-Raising recommends these topical but atypical courses:

Futuristic Scientistics: A truly avant-garde course featuring cultural disfunctionalism, knowledge implosion, hormonal influences on resistance movements, and the impact of LSD on ESP. Input is slated from experts in necromantics, signifiers, and psychokinesis.

Problems in Non-Knowledge: A real groovy preview of next year's educational hallucinations. The course will transcend logic and rationality, drawing instead on probablistic indeterminates and post-fractal chaos to refine the art of statistical legerdemain. A gigantic bonfire will climax the course, fed by this year's ed psych papers.

Studies in Campus Chaos: A turned-on use of homeopathy to treat campus-now problems, such as the need to teach students, pay professors, and gut the administration. The course will confront the publish-or-perish syndrome, student *Kinderspiel*, and psychosocial aposiopesis. Emphasis will be on good vibes and telling-it-like-it-is.

Educational Granitics: A hard-nosed, sesquipedalian ventilation of dithyrambic notions like how often should professors be mentally examined? Should philosophers be tenured?

What pedagogies are kitsch? Course is especially valuable for whomping up rhetoric sans perscrutination. The professor is required to trip out with his students. An account of same constitutes the term paper.

The Researcher's Art: A fearless practicum unlocking such hermetics as how to hype grants, write gobledygook, do research–requiring–further–research, create statistical paralepsis, test tests for good testing, etc. The approach will be prepositivist and postmodern with a bias toward aesculapean pathology.

Fads and Fantasies: A really cool introduction to academic stasis conducted by wild-eyed students for starry-eyed professors, making everyone hip to such conceptual anodynes as sensitization, instant gratification, touchy–feely, and learning facilitation. Stress will be on relating-to, doing-your-own-thing, and making-out.

Quiddities and Quoddities: A hands–on, apocalyptic seminar in scholarly futility, featuring the ultimate in the educational Theater of the Absurd.

February 1971

13

What Research Is Worth Most ?

pplying strict scientific methods to a nonscientific subject is like using literary criticism to do physics. Since education is largely off limits to science, educational studies using these methods are pointless. What methods should we use?

First, we should theorize; that is, seek fundamental explanations. One way of doing so is to propose models—explanatory insights expressed in sets of propositions—and deduce their consequences. History, literary studies, and anthropology yield the best insights for models of education, and they should be analyzed philosophically. Any aspect of education can be modeled: institutions, processes, curricula, methods, organization, administration.

We may also form basic principles and pursue their implications, as many great thinkers have done. While it is essential to analyze the concepts occurring in these principles (mind, equality, growth, motivation, etc.), the prime task is to develop powerful theses that include them.

We must distinguish between the content of education— the knowledge taught and learned—and the process of education—the acts of teaching and learning it. In a technological society gadgets and techniques invade the educational process, tending to distort and sometimes determine content, as when math and science may be reduced to rote learning by

CAI and programmed instruction.

Although education varies from one society to another, it makes sense to focus on those features that most educational systems have in common. Too much research in education is unrelated to basic principles or to any significant aspects of education that may be universal.

Since education seeks to develop character as well as intellect, research findings should be evaluated morally before they are acted on. It is not enough to "find" that, *e.g.*, CAI is more "efficient" than lecturing. We must consider whether it makes students better people (*i.e.*, more thoughtful, more concerned, more interested in the world).

Education primarily is one of the humanities, like philosophy, history, and literature, all of which have guiding principles but little logical structure. These, not physics and mathematics, should be the models for the study of education. Educationists should seek the basic principles that give their discipline unity and coherence. There is no need to aim at a logical hierarchy of propositions.

The first task of research is to formulate these principles. In fact, all educationists should take an equivalent of the Hippocratic Oath: *Only publish work that is related to basic educational principles.*

May 1972

26

14

Farewell, GSE!
Hail, EdCom and Studessors!

n response to overwhelming student-professor demand for greater community consciousness, the Graduate School of Education faculty adopted the following recommendations:

◆ The GSE will be renamed the Education Commune (EdCom) in keeping with the "new consciousness." Collegiality yields to community.

◆ The categories of student and professor will be eliminated by the introduction of a new mode of being, "studessorship," which will revolutionize campus life.

◆ Deans, chairmen, and their assistants will be replaced by studessors representing the Commune.

◆ All nonacademics will be replaced by studessors doing their own thing.

◆ All classrooms will be converted to private offices, share and share alike. Tents in the quad will serve as community living quarters. The Evaluation Center will become a studessor lounge.

◆ Now that students are to be their own teachers, and teach-

27

ers their own students, a non-negotiable demand will be submitted to the Legislature stipulating a minimum salary of $100 a week plus benefits as mandated by the International Union of Studessors.

♦ No applicant over 30 will be admitted to the EdCom, and studessors will be required to complete their work by their 31st birthday.

♦ A community of the Commune will be appointed to draft a resolution dissolving the Board of Regents.

♦ All University departments will be invited to follow the lead of the Education Commune. Special revolutionary committees will be formed in such Schools as Medicine, Law, and Engineering, where the knowledge gap between students and professors has been grossly exaggerated.

♦ Grading, evaluating, and record keeping will be replaced by studessor self–evaluation. Job references will be written by applicants themselves, so as to make them truly authentic.

♦ Students and professors opposed to the Commune will be indoctrinated at special retreats, failing which they will be exiled.

January 1971

15

Research Proves? Shows? Demonstrates?

hich is correct? None. Ninety–five percent of current educational research neither proves, shows, nor demonstrates anything scientific. Much of It is actually harmful.

When I read of the money spent on educational research and then look at my tax returns, I reach for a tranquilizer. I have just perused a piece of "survey research." It could have been done by any undergraduate studying poll-taking. Yet it was submitted as evidence for a promotion.

Researchers like to point to "the weight of the evidence," meaning that if their evidence weighs twice as much as another's, it's twice as good. They also weigh in with statistics, which "validate" whatever their users want them to. They then weigh down their reports with loads of references, most of which neither they nor their readers ever consult. This farce passes for "creative scholarship."

Let's talk sense. The main task of empirical research is to propose testable models derived from higher-level theories. For example, research on human behavior is or should be based on a theory of man; curriculum research, on a theory of knowledge; organization and administration, on a theory of politics. In fact, all educational research should relate to a theory of education. Anyone who finds such research, please let me know!

Some recent research claims to "get inside" such movements as "school decentralization," calling them truly democratic. They are not. Equating decentralization with democracy is a "category mistake" (as Gilbert Ryle put it). There is no logical, empirical, or political link between these concepts. If you disbelieve this, tell me why most democracies have centralized educational systems.

The other day a colleague informed me that the sociology of learning "lags behind" the psychology of learning. Fact is, neither has yet been formulated. Rest easy, sociologists! Make sure, however, that your future research rests on a theory of society. How much ed psych research is based on a theory of mind? Practically none.

Several key issues remain to be resolved. How does university research differ from research done elsewhere? What happens to the "findings"? Who uses them? What difference have they made? If they are merely filed, why should they count toward promotion? Why indeed!

November 72

16

The Med School Comparison

It's fashionable these days to compare medicine and education as professions. It is said that if education is to become a true profession, like medicine, it deserves equal respect and compensation. In fact, the two professions are quite dissimular.

Medical research uses objective standards, relies on measurement, and depends on the natural sciences, above all physiology. What disciplines support the practice of education? That depends on your concept of education. Have you ever defined it?

Terms in medicine are precisely defined. Not so in education. With terms like "mind," "motivation," "development," "learning," every educator rolls his own meaning. Ed research borrows heavily from the humanities and the human sciences. Instead of coordinating this knowledge, educationists divide it up. To each his own!

Medical diagnosis and prescription are largely objective. Different diseases have recognized symptoms and recognized treatments. In education, on the other hand, there is endless disagreement over teaching methods, curricula, even the goals of schooling. Ever heard of a lay board tossing out medical texts?

Doctors use serums, syringes, scalpels, operating tables, x-ray labs, precisely calibrated tools. Teachers make do with hit-or-miss devices like computers that say "Hi!" and projec-

31

tors that break down to Bronx cheers. There is talk of teaching "labs," but that's merely to impress agencies addled enough to believe that these resemble biology labs. Furthermore, most physicians engage in private practice, whereas most educationists are institutionalized.

Medical science may not be as exact as we would like, but education is no science at all. We should drop the pretense that it is and stop squandering scarce resources on a chimera.

The good news? Most professional educationists have the PhD, a higher sobriquet than the MD. I never lose an opportunity to tell my physician friends that I outrank them academically.

December 1972

17

The Education of Women

A colleague has reminded me that in a series of essays I had published on "The Idea of the University" I had said little about the influence of women. Here is a digest of my thoughts. Women had to fight harder than men for the right to teach and learn. In the United States, one of the first to break the barrier was Mary Lyon (1797-1849).

Brought up the hard way, Miss Lyon had to work for her schooling and so had more reason to press for reform than most of her contemporaries. She strove to raise the education of women "to the highest level" and give them a college "second to none...not even Harvard." In 1837 she opened Mount Holyoke Seminary, dedicating it not only to the education of women but more significantly to the advancement of learning.

Like other workers for women's rights, Mary Lyon sought to prove to the world that the female brain is every bit as good as the male. Given an equal chance, she insisted, girls are the intellectual equal of boys. In her day such notions were heresy, and neither passion nor evidence could move public opinion.

Despite snubs and sneers, Mary Lyon fulfilled her mission. By mid–century Mt. Holyoke was not only accepted, it had become a model for other women's colleges.

I have space for only one more woman educator. Alice

33

Freeman Palmer (1855–1902) figured in one of the most delightful incidents in educational history. In 1882 at age 26 she was offered the presidency of Wellesley College. Saying she was too young and that the office was too much for one person, she agreed to accept if the students would discipline themselves and leave her free for general administration. The students jumped at the opportunity, Palmer took the position, and serious indiscipline ceased.

Thanks to the work of women, coeducation inched forward. Oberlin adopted it in 1833, but it was not until twenty years later that Horace Mann enrolled girls at Antioch. Even then, most private colleges viewed coeducation as a threat to virtue and a violation of the laws of nature. Cornell was an exception. In 1872 President Andrew Dickson White welcomed girls as equal to boys (or nearly so). Dickson quoted Plato in his defense, but his motive was hardly Platonic. Like other leaders of private colleges, he needed endowments, and enrolling girls was a good way to get them.

Coeducation, then, was not adopted out of masculine magnanimity or even to beautify the campus. Coeducation meant more cash. It still does. When Harvard, Yale, Princeton, and Dartmouth dissolved their monasteries, they expected the parents of girls to reward them handsomely for the "sacrifice" they had made.

January 1973

18

Ah, Progress, May We Swell Thy Name!

The Graduate School of Education has over 250 personnel of various kinds. The latest full-time academic FTE count is 53.5. Thus the ratio is one full-time professor to about five others.

The number of deans (associates and assistants) has risen to nine. What department in the University can boast such an impressive array of professional stewards?

Assisting this diaconate are three area chairmen, 17 specialization heads, 15 committee chairmen, a dozen directors of this and that (TEL, vocational education, R & D Center, Policy Studies, etc.), and a long line of poohbahs, for a conservative total of 65. The GSE now has more chiefs than Indians.

Class enrollments are chaotic, numbering from a few to a few hundred. Without Jim Bruno's equalization formulas, the disorder would be worse. Professors continue to cut their teaching hours, some struggling through as many as one course per term. Office hours are dimly posted, the subtext being "Catch Me If You Can."

Knowledge seems to vary inversely as the number of FTE faculty positions assigned to it. History, philosophy, anthropology have one FTE apiece. Sociology has three, and psychology, a dozen. In addition, an ever-increasing number of minicourses appear and they impart more and more about less and less. They are offered at the whim of the professor, but are always said to "meet the needs" of students.

Paper-pushing expands everywhere. The process starts with one of the higher deans and descends to lower deans, who get the academics to fill out forms for the nonacademics, who then send students back to the academics for information that in the meantime has been updated. Budgets show a steady rise in the cost and quantity of paper used, and that should be proof enough of consistent progress in the realm of paper-pushing.

In securing research funds we are without rival. The Regents recently rewarded our achievement by reducing the recommended assignment of FTEs from 61 to 53, on the grounds that the GSE is already awash in gifts and grants. However, the Regents now promise a bonus of one FTE if we provide them with another million out of our research funds.

The above account of our affairs reveals not only overt psychotic but covert suicidal tendencies, for among us are some honest researchers who deny the worth of it all. There is no proof, they say, that anything we do here improves education. Our progress, then, is defined in terms of the amount of paper used, not the results achieved.

March 1973

19

The Foreign Language Bugaboo

In order to meet the criticism of foreign language requirements for the PhD and to make the study of the language more fruitful, I propose that one or more courses be created for the study of education in the language of the home country.

For example, Course X could be one of our breadth courses, and it would study educational ideas and events described in publications in Spanish, French, German, or some other language. Passing one of these courses would satisfy both the foreign language and breadth course requirements.

These courses would be taught by Graduate School of Education faculty, assisted by instructors from the language departments. They could be considered courses in comparative education or anthropology of education. They could be cross-referenced.

I see all kinds of possibilities. A Spanish class could travel to Mexico and hobnob with Mexican educators. (My students and I did this annually.) Mexican educators could return the visit. (They did so.) Foreign students, teachers, and others could address our classes. For a real thrill, students could study foreign language translations of publications by GSE professors...on education, of course.

Here is an opportunity not only to innovate constructively but to make our University more universal. Not only language but also culture would be added to our courses, and our School would become more cosmopolitan.

Too much of our work is provincial, geared to the needs of local schools, needs which are better met in teacher training institutions, state universities, and other post-secondary schools. We ought to distinguish ourselves from these institutions. We should seek knowledge and teach it, not to serve California alone, or even the nation, but nations and cultures everywhere.

Do I speak from experience? Have I taught such courses? Yes, indeed. My students did not view their language examination as an artificial hurdle. They learned more than language. Let's therefore shun fashions for once and adopt something that will not go out of style. If adopting this program means that some courses would have to be dropped, there being only so much room in the curriculum, I would be happy to name a few. They are not courses at all but topics and in a decade they'll be forgotten.

April 1973

20

The Secret Cost of Grants

n *Phi Delta Kappan*, June 1973, Michael Chiappetta (Indiana University) revealed some startling facts about what it costs universities to obtain grants. While no sweeping conclusions can be drawn from his article, it made me think of our own grant mania and our ever-shrinking *Lebenswelt* in Moore Hall. What further space can we assign to subsidized research? How about dismantling another classroom and another privy?

I may be a philosopher, but I also am a businessman, and I began to wonder how much money has been invested in faculty time, energy, and related costs that results in no grants at all...or how this investment compares with money we have actually received and spent. (Note that grant money is funneled through the University, which takes its cut.)

Research indeed is valuable, but if experience teaches us anything, it is that most experimental/behavioral research in education is unproductive. Either it refines the obvious or caters to fads. There is no well–confirmed scientific theory of education. As for prediction, a gypsy fortune–teller, for a slight grease of the palm, would perform as well as our researchers and probably better.

It is important, of course, to learn how some children behave with other children under carefully defined conditions. It is important to know that Mississippi spends more of its per capita wealth on education than California does. But this kind of information can be unearthed by intelligent lay people with the help of insurance actuaries. We don't need a top-flight university for this.

If School of Education faculties were to cut their research in half, would education really suffer? How well has education fared under the avalanche of data unleashed by post-war research? It might have done better without any research at all. It could hardly have done worse. If faculty halved their research, they could double their teaching loads and save the universities pots of money.

Chiappetta's article really made me think. Most educational research is just another drain on the nation's dwindling resources. Maybe I could get a grant to prove this hypothesis. Or I might write to my Congressman. Why did I have to read that article? I just can't get it out of my mind.

October 1973

21

Bill Buckley's Question

ome time ago on "Firing Line" William F. Buckley, Jr., concerned that educational research had produced so few scientific facts, gave Wilson Riles, California's Superintendent of Public Instruction, a list of six prime factors in any educational endeavor:

- ◆ Teacher skill
- ◆ Student attitude
- ◆ Parental influence
- ◆ Learning environment
- ◆ Student intelligence
- ◆ Socio–economic conditions

Buckley asked Riles to rate these factors on a 100-point scale according to scientific findings.

Riles hesitated and asked Buckley to repeat the question. He did. Riles replied that he could not rate the factors quantitatively. We do not have the evidence, he said. All factors are important, but for different reasons, in different amounts, and in different environments.

How right he was! After spending millions to measure educational priorities, we still have no definitive answers. And we never shall. Neither quantitative nor scientific research will ever solve the really important problems of education. "Evalua-

41

tion" makes no contribution at all.

Some educationists are convinced that if we ask enough people what they think, we will get the answers we want. If most respondents rate a single factor highest, that factor will be the most important. The factor with the least votes will be the least important. This exercise, if done in a university, goes by the name of "survey research"; if by a lay organization, "polltaking." The results are the same. True knowledge is said to be validated by democratic vote. That people change their minds from day to day does not invalidate findings. We simply await the next poll. And another grant.

Why do educational researchers persist in their errors? For several reasons:

- ◆ This is the way they were trained in graduate school.
- ◆ They think that their methods can "prove" something.
- ◆ They can't do anything else.
- ◆ Their publications fatten their bios.
- ◆ They do not realize they are deluding themselves.

Will someone able to answer Bill Buckley's question please step forward and be recognized?

> *In the universal Hall of Fame*
> *I'll gladly place your lustrous name.*
> *And if we then researchers tame,*
> *To Buckley I will send your name!*

January 1974

42

22

Research in Teacher Education and the Pursuit of a Chimera

We now have a grant from the Spencer Foundation to define the nature and scope of research in teacher education. Our Teacher Education Laboratory (TEL) is given a year to research this topic. What kind of research will TEL do to define research?

TEL needs neither the money nor the year, for the answers can be found in the literature and they can be produced in a week by any competent scholar. The Spencer Foundation is unaware of the futility of its projects, and grantees continue to be seduced into thinking they can solve teaching problems with the methods of the behavioral sciences.

For teaching is neither a discipline nor a science. It is primarily an art and a technique, and you either have it or you don't...as countless wise men have told us since Confucius and Socrates. There are no laws of teaching behavior, anymore than there are of behavior on Wall Street (which would close down if there were). If TEL nonetheless uses the methods of the human sciences, I predict flat failure by the end of the year.

If, on the other hand, TEL respects the nature of teaching and turns instead to history, philosophy, and literary studies, it will succeed in less than a year. What method should it follow? A combination of documentary research, philosophic analysis,

43

literary study, biography, and interviews with teachers.
How can TEL improve its program?

◆ Recruit promising students from the freshman and sophomore classes... Get 'em while they're young!

◆ Give them professors who are exemplary teachers.

◆ Insist on intellectual attainment, not practice in adaptation.

◆ Find the most talented teachers in public and private schools, and invite each to take two or three of our students as apprentices.

No accumulation of gadgets, recipes, artful dodges, tricks of the trade, modules, mini–lessons, and other artifices ever will substitute for great teaching. This means that we must study education first and teaching second. Assessment instruments and evaluation procedures will amount to nothing unless they are based on an understanding of Education as a discipline.

A decade ago this Graduate School of Education squandered three years and $3 million in a futile attempt to define teacher education. Will we ever learn?

March 1975

23

Yet Another Five-Year Plan (1976-81)

A t it again! Fortunately, this Report is relatively free of jargon. Its literary style is tolerable. It is better conceptualized. Any report which assumes that education is primarily a moral enterprise has to be taken seriously.

To its credit, the Report:

◆ Endorses "an examination of beliefs regarding the nature of man, knowledge, and the good society."

◆ Advocates more awareness of the assumptions governing research.

◆ Questions the values underlying accountability and evaluation.

◆ Recommends more outreach to other disciplines.

◆ Insists that "if specialists are incapable of teaching courses in which the principles taught have broad application, then we have the wrong specialists."

◆ Criticizes the current overlap among courses.

There are several flaws.

◆ Policy, a set of statements specifying a course of action, is undefined and no action is specified.

◆ Some historical facts are garbled, and this is inexcusable in a document claiming that "we should develop a deep awareness of our historical traditions."

45

◆ Contrary to the Report, there was more unity in the Graduate School of Education 20 years ago. We had no areas and no specializations, even though the number of faculty members was the same.

◆ The proposed basic study program is largely a repeat of what we had 20 years ago.

◆ While claiming that education is largely a normative enterprise, the Report is overwhelmingly technical in its emphasis, being obsessed with practical outcomes and measures of achievement.

Two misleading statements appear:

◆ Brain research is credited with a message for education. In fact, brain research has nothing to tell education, and we should not pretend that it does. The articles in the *UCLA Educator* on the implications of brain research are a shameful display of ignorance.

◆ The Report also states that in certain circumstances "we should reject opportunities to increase our extramural resources, since they too often deflect us from our true mission." Fine! But doing so will require a lot more courage than I have seen around here. It will cut off most of the largesse to which we are accustomed. It also will put an end to the Teacher Education Laboratory in its present form.

Like most reports, this one tells us what we should add with little mention of what to subtract. It also contains the usual odd comments, entered to satisfy individual committee members. When a symphony is composed by a group, a *vox vagans* is bound to be heard, in tune or not.

The Report says it is not a challenge to the present mission and organization of the GSE. Why isn't it? Both mission and organization need to be challenged. Despite its caution, however, this Report has taken a small step in the right direction.

May 1976

24

Split-Brain Studies: A Trap for the Unwary

ashion-followers in education have found a new passion. Several Graduate School of Education faculty are lecturing on split–brain theory. Some have written articles. At least one is preparing a book. A recent issue of the *UCLA Educator* was devoted entirely to the topic, without mentioning a single fact of any relevance to education. It is time to stop this charade. Researching on the frontiers of knowledge is one thing, claiming to have discovered them is another.

Barely a decade old, split-brain theory is changing fast. The two sides of the brain, it seems, are closely connected and one side cannot function without the other. The right side now packs most linguistic skills, but the dominant left often suppresses them. There is more to the tale, and the conclusion is a long way off. A brain-computer hookup will take at least 50 years, says Adam Reed, one of our most sanguine researchers. Without one, we shan't discover much.

Some experts claim that split-brain theory outdates Freud, Piaget, and Skinner, who "ignored" the brain. This theory, they say, will revolutionize our understanding of human development. But does the source of our thinking lie in the neocortex, the hippocampus, the limbic region, or what? Where does a thought go once we express it? Fact is, our current knowledge is limited to the physiology of certain regions of the brain observed under highly restricted conditions. Without a unified theory of the brain, without a scientific theory of the mind–brain relation, any inference from brain research to education is sheer speculation.

Brain research must of course continue. It actually can be amusing. We now know, or think we do, that the right side gets drunk first, since apparently it has a "lower threshold for disruption." Some researchers are investigating bird brains (though not their own) before, during, and after birth. It is also rumored that politicos on the right are secretly funding research to disprove cerebral domination from the left.

What does current brain research offer education? Nothing of any consequence. Anyone who says it does is a sciolist. I recently discussed this topic with a senior member of UCLA's Brain Research Center. "Why come here?" he asked. "Your people in Education seem to know more than we do!" He was being ironic, of course.

September 1977

25

What's All This about Sociobiology?

rendy educationists have latched onto something called sociobiology, a bold—if misguided—attempt to unite a science (biology) with a pseudoscience (sociology).

This unlikely hybrid, feeding on a dozen specialties, claims to find precedents in animal life for a wide range of human behavior. Shedding logic and sense, starry-eyed educationists have followed suit, citing animal roots for educational practices.

These converts ignore differences in the methods used by the two forms of inquiry. Only with difficulty can knowledge claims established with one set of methods (biological) be made to yield conclusions reached with another set (sociological). The two groups of propositions clash rather than consort. Even if this were not the case, the drive to make sociology a science has collapsed, and no serious effort has been mounted to turn biology into a social study.

Sociobiology abounds in unsubstantiated claims, such as the assertion that some animals behave "altruistically." But an animal cannot favor group interest over its own instincts unless it is conscious of doing so, and animals aren't self-conscious. Yet suppose sociobiologists are right, that humans are programmed to do much that we thought had to be learned. It does not follow that we should educate them solely to obey our genes. If we humans, in fact, have an animal inheritance, we still must decide whether to act on that inheritance or suppress it.

Sociobiologists cannot answer the pressing questions of education. What moral behavior is learned and what is innate? Sociobiology can't tell us. Should subject matter come first or the felt needs of the child? No help from sociobiology. Forced bussing—yes or no? Sociobiologists line up on both sides.

On principle, we can support efforts to improve education by using knowledge from other disciplines. This knowledge must, however, be verifiable, applicable, and useful. Reciprocally, other disciplines should turn to education to refine their use of concepts like learning, teaching, memorizing, evaluating, and motivating. There is no evidence that sociobiologists look to educationists for help in anything they do.

April 1979

26

Multicultural Education: Boon or Boondoggle?

ager to polish their image (and attract more funds), bilingual educators have adopted "bi-cultural" and now "multicultural" education. Their avowed purpose is to acquaint students with America's many cultures.

A worthy goal but a tall order. Advocates do not realize what must done to meet it. Our Graduate School of Education, for instance, has virtually abandoned the study of foreign languages, and not many students will let the study of other cultures interfere with their pursuit of marginal specialties.

Few American public school teachers can present their own culture adequately, let alone other people's. Only 5% of them have taken intercultural studies, and less than 15% have pursued a foreign language beyond the second year. Moreover, proficiency in a language doesn't guarantee that one can teach its culture.

Is multicultural education just another boondoggle? Its advocates are calling for reforms, and education may be diluted yet again, for there is a limit to what we can do.

Will history repeat itself? In the 1930s reformers called for the "needs" curriculum to be made "an integral part of the education process at all levels." In the 1940s as much was sought for the "life adjustment" curriculum; in the 1950s, for the "core" curriculum; in the 1960s, for "teacher-proof" materials; in the

1970s, for social reconstruction programs. Where are they now? The needs curriculum failed because needs could not be adequately specified. Life adjustment faded because few could agree on the meaning of life and, whatever life meant, few were found adjusted to it. Core fell by the way because too many cores competed for recognition. Teacher-proof materials ceased to be teacher-proof when used by teachers. The details of social reconstruction remain undecided.

The multicultural curriculum must not be allowed to suffer the same fate. The idea is too important. Can it be achieved? Yes. We have the resources, the staff, and the leadership. What we need is a formal program and the will to see it through.

Training for multicultural education cannot be limited to a fifth year. We will have to reach into the lower division and find recruits prepared to spend several years studying languages and cultures.

This is not too much to expect. Like it or not, we are a nation of many social and ethnic groups, each proud of its achievements, each contributing to the whole and expecting recognition. Programs in multicultural education will require a new breed of dedicated, talented professionals. Until they appear, the programs will remain inert.

October 1979

27

Teacher Education
and Foundations of Education

There is no end to proposals for teacher education. There is no progress either, only change. For teaching is an art and a passion, not a list of do's and don'ts, and the best of teachers must be born before they can be "trained."

What shall a teacher know? As a teacher, not too much beyond what she has to teach. As a scholar, all that the brain will hold. As a person, whatever is needed for self-fulfillment.

What use are Foundations courses? To the teacher as teacher, very little. To the person and the scholar, very much. They introduce the student to the study of Education as a discipline on a par with other disciplines, yet all the more important because Education, not teaching, has become a major.

Who should teach Foundations? Chiefly historians and philosophers, for, like Education itself, these disciplines encompass all others.

What is research in teaching? A misnomer, unless pursued as part of the discipline of Education. What is practice in teaching? It is selective emulation—the acceptance or rejection of other people's teaching critically observed. By what criteria? Those derived from the study of Education together with one's own intuition and values.

What do "objective tests of efficient teaching" reveal? All

sorts of conflicting findings, none conclusive. There are no agreed-on definitions of "objective," "efficient," or "teaching." Of "tests," only the tester has the "answers."

What are the latest "innovations" in teaching? There aren't any, as any serious history student knows. There are only variations on time-honored practices.

What do we know about "evaluation" in teaching? Not much more than we did before we squandered $10 million on it.

Is all our labor, then, in vain? Most of it, yes, because it's based on the sciences, which have contributed practically nothing to our understanding of education. When education-ists draw on the true disciplines for *our* discipline—history, phi-losophy, anthropology, and literary studies—worthwhile work will begin.

January 1981

28

Deconstructionism–1

t takes a lot of nerve to "define" a movement that deconstructs definitions. But since the movement is within the gates, I suggest we regard it as a critique of all absolutes, universals, systematic philosophies, and even conceptual analysis. Like other forms of poststructuralism, deconstructionism asserts that since no knowledge is final, concepts like freedom, equality, and individuality are "unreliable" (undefinable). Moral notions such as good and evil, right and wrong, altruism and selfishness disintegrate under the deconstructionist assault.

What is being done with the rubble? A few decons are putting some of it back together, but most are happy pulling ideas apart—not to reconnect them, but to expose false assumptions, linguistic inadequacies, and, above all, inner contradictions.

The master concept of deconstructionism is *text*, or any analagous message. A text is sovereign, not the author. A text does not have a single, prechosen meaning. On the contrary, its words create whatever meanings are compatible with them. (The words mean whatever they can mean, not just what they were chosen to mean.) An author's intention dissolves in the play of "signifiers," which generate meanings independently. Any text contains "unreliabilities" that subvert its apparent meaning, so that behind the latter another meaning unfolds. But this meaning too is at variance with itself, so the process of deconstructing may continue indefinitely. What does a text mean? It means whatever any deconstructionist says it does.

May decons read into the text whatever meaning they like? No. Free–wheeling is out. The task is to uncover asymmetry, irreconcilability, and the interference of words with meaning. In particular, it is to undermine the positivist assumption, still driving much research in education and the human sciences, that inquiry can reach truth.

What does deconstructionism hold for education? We must give up the search for universal theories, fixed principles, large-scale taxonomies, grand curricular designs, standardized tests. We must abandon cookbook procedures. Teachers and students must become "interpreters" of texts, disclosing the meanings that escaped their authors. They must deconstruct the works they read.

Some decons call for a "critical pedagogy," based on the "pedagogy of the oppressed," a "recuperated" Marxism, and a critique of culture. They urge educators to become "critical social agents...knowing how to live contingently...yet at the same time with the courage to take a stand on issues of human suffering, domination, and oppression." Stay tuned!

February 1990

29

Deconstructionism-II

The heart of critical pedagogy is the proposal for an "emancipatory curriculum," enabling students to criticize and transcend the "disabling conditions" of mass culture. Students must learn to "challenge those voices of accommodation which celebrate a uniform public morality and a monolithic political reality based on labor market imperatives and cultural consensus." Teachers "must examine the contextual conditions of their classrooms and communities, so that they can construct their own pedagogical models of teacher and student empowerment."

There's a political ideology at work here. I have yet to find a single educational deconstructionist, poststructuralist, discourse theorist, or critical pedagogist on the political right. Why do you suppose this is? Chief guru Jacques Derrida says a few rightists are infiltrating literature and philosophy, and he doesn't like it. Why do you suppose he doesn't?

How does deconstruction work? Take the statement, "All men are born free and equal." Is this statement true? Does it apply to everyone everywhere? How can the new-born be free? If all men are born equal, why are some more talented than others? Since neither freedom nor equality can be absolute, this entire statement, which purports to be canonical, is absurd. Or take the statement, "Society should meet the needs of children." What society? What needs? All children? What

57

needs should not be met? This statement, grammatically correct, well–structured, well-meaning, is meaningless. The question is not, What does a text mean? but Whence does meaning appear?

Now consider that hypnotic concept, "educational reform." Decons would delight in demolishing it. Who wants reform and why? Whose education? How will we know when we've got it?

Deconstructionism is literary criticism *à outrance*. But why pulverize such beautiful lines as Shakespeare's "My bounty is as boundless as the sea,/ My love is as deep"? These hermeticists belabor their points in arcane, rebarbative detail. Granted, the *avant-garde* always seems outrageous. Yet other excesses, once applauded, have spent themselves, like raw behaviorism, logical positivism, and Anglo-American surrealism.

Decons seem unsure as to their future—"what is to be," as they put it—though confident of the "valorization" of their work today. For an assessment of the movement, I quote Mark C. Taylor of Williams College: "The issues of deconstructionism are of more than academic interest.... If we are to move on, it cannot be with the imperious certainty we once believed we possessed but only with a salutary uncertainty keeping us open to what we can never fully understand."

Me? I like the derring–do, the quest for hidden meanings. But I dislike the rejection of independent realities.

March 1990

30

Course Proliferation: The Dumbing of Education

have just looked at the Graduate School of Education course catalog, and what I see is unbelievable. There are over 500 course offerings. Whom are we trying to impress? In all of Education there isn't enough knowledge to sustain even half that number.

The courses are organized in five Divisions, but it is hard to see how some courses belong where they are. The Divisions are academically meaningless. They seem contrived, apparently the outcome of power plays rather than concern for subject matter.

Take, for example, the Research Division. Since all faculty do research, and since their researches vary, this category represents nothing intellectually unique. Why not list these courses by subject matter? In consideration of the energy put into educational research and the money invested, the payoff has been negligible. So, instead of setting up this superfluous Division, why not create just one course to demonstrate the value and usefulness of certain research findings? That would be a real challenge.

Or consider the Ed Psych Division, which lists over 50 courses. Why not halve this number by combining courses and telescoping content? The new lineup would supply a solid, year-long course in medical psychiatry (taught by a Med School professor) and a course in the history of ed psych. The former would provide essential physiological knowledge; the latter, a sorely needed account of how philosophic and other assumptions have steered research (*e.g.*, associationism, introspectionism, behaviorism, and functionalism). "Give me any statement in psychology," said Carl Jung, "and I'll give you its opposite."

Some courses seem to duplicate offerings in other Divisions. Some are not courses at all, but topics. If courses or topics focus on race, culture, or language, pass the material to a good ethnologist, cultural anthropologist, or whoever will handle it in truly scholarly fashion. Send some political and social issues to political and social scientists for analysis before trying to draw educational implications.

Over the years I have spent much time studying syllabi and reading published research. I must repeat that until educationists learn to appreciate the logical order of subject matter and the academic relevance of their research, the study of education will remain an object of derision. Is this our legacy to teachers?

Course proliferation and overspecialization will only reinforce the negative image we now portray.

April 1990

31

four Endowed Chairs

ost faculty are aware of my award of four endowed Chairs, but in view of current thinking about the future of the Graduate School of Education, I would like to outline the nature of the endowment and the reasons for it.

The Chairs express my conviction that we must encourage increased interdisciplinary activity and foster the study of Education as an autonomous discipline.

As a *theoretical* discipline, Education is primarily one of the humanities and only secondarily a social science with a minimum of quantitative analysis. As a *practical* discipline, Education examines and makes recommendations on all aspects of schooling: administration, curriculum, pedagogy, community relations, professional training.

What are the humanities? They include those branches of knowledge, such as history, philosophy, literature, language, and art, that are concerned with human thought and culture rather than with natural science processes. The study of Education belongs essentially in the humanities because its subject is the formation—intellectual, moral, and emotional—of human beings. Like other humanities it offers facts, ideas, and theories about what it is to be human. Scientific data and generalizations are useful to the extent that they respect the uniqueness and diversity of human beings.

Chair holders will see Education as essentially a theoretical study. They will enrich their joint disciplines through the research and teaching it inspires.

These Chairs also provide support for graduate assistants, post–doctoral fellows, research, and special projects. They are designed to inspire and reward peak academic performance, and provide a unique opportunity to invest permanently in the work of higher education.

August 1990

32

Chair in Philosophy and Education

hen I first proposed the Chairs, the Executive Vice Chancellor asked me to state what I hoped they would achieve. He then submitted my proposal to the five Departments (Anthropology, Education, English, History, Philosophy) for their approval. Below is my response on the relation between Education and Philosophy:

From philosophers, educationists can learn in more depth how to:

◆ Analyze and clarify the concepts and principles in terms of which educational issues are explored and understood. What do these concepts and principles imply? Where do they conflict? What meaningfully can be said about them?

◆ Examine the assumptions about knowledge, values, human nature, teaching, discipline, authority, etc., that underlie educational theories and practices.

◆ Assess the claims and methods of empirical studies in education, exposing faulty reasoning, conceptual confusion, and methodological flaws.

◆ Make broad recommendations on specific issues, such as

school choice, curriculum reform, moral education, equality of opportunity, and evaluation procedures.

◆ Expound and assess the educational thought of great philosophers, past and present, all of whom have much to say on the subject.

From the educationists, the philosophers, in turn can:

◆ Extend their theories into developing implications for educational thought and practice.

◆ Check that the analyses of general concepts (*e.g.*, freedom, equality, rights, responsibility) do justice to their meanings in education.

◆ Find case studies of teaching/learning, curriculum design, classroom discipline, etc., to test the relevance of their reflections.

◆ Trace educational analogues in works of philosophy, thereby illustrating the influence of the educational experience on philosophic thought.

◆ Offer informed advice on the teaching of philosophy.

The philosophy of education is on a par with the philosophic study of history, science, literature, religion, psychology, politics, etc. This Chair should contribute to the appreciation and growth of this field.

September 1990

33

Why a Chair in Anthropology and Education?

I endowed this Chair because anthropology is the broadest of the human sciences and the most sensitive to other cultures. Whereas psychology and sociology largely reflect American values and the study of Western educational systems, anthropology scans education across the globe and consciously brackets the values of the investigator. It is a crucial discipline for a multicultural nation in a multipolar world.

Anthropologists make these contributions to the study of Education:

◆ They examine the immense influence of cultural beliefs and values on all phases of education: teaching methods, learning styles, modes of discipline, and manifest and hidden curricula.

◆ They identify common elements in the world's educational systems, elements such as tradition, teacher authority, moral and religious training, student socialization, administration, and parent-teacher relations.

◆ They investigate such controversial issues as racial and ethnic identity, language acquisition and use, bilingual education, and the cultural conflicts faced by minorities in schools where majority values prevail.

◆ They inquire into the cultures of institutions involved in education: family, community, school, bureaucracy, funding agencies, and pressure groups.

Research in education enriches anthropology by:

◆ Applying anthropological theories, asking, for example, whether education confirms Leslie White's theses that innovations are new combinations of old culture elements and that the degree of change in any field reflects the evolution of the culture as a whole.

◆ Proposing hypotheses that reach beyond education, such as John Ogbu's school performance–based distinction between immigrant and non–immigrant minority groups.

◆ Exploring the effects of education on the wider culture, as in the influence of content-oriented Japanese education and the inquiry-oriented American education on the distinctive personality types fostered by these two cultures.

◆ Refining the methods of applied anthropology, *e.g.*, combining an anthropological description of problems with the proposal of educational solutions.

October 1990

34

Why a Chair in Literature and Education?

created this Chair because I believe that no subject does more for the education student than the study of literature. Where else do we find such deep knowledge of human beings embodied in such varied characters and presented with such emotional and intellectual power?

How does the study of literature help us understand Education?

◆ By appealing to the feelings and senses as well as the intellect, literature involves us more fully than other approaches in the experiences it depicts (those of the young teacher Ursula Brandwin in D.H. Lawrence's novel *The Rainbow*).

◆ By compelling us to identify with literary characters (J. D. Salinger's Holden Caulfield, John Updike's Rabbit Angstrom), literature invites us to enter more sympathetically into their lives than into lives studied scientifically.

◆ Literature reveals more profoundly and poignantly than other subjects the moral conflicts of teachers, students, parents, and others, as in the responses of the characters to the murder of a student in Mario Vargas–Llosa's *Time of the Hero*.

67

◆ Literature treats education from many points of view and in a range of literary forms: novel, short story, poem, memoir (George Orwell's *Such, Such Were the Joys*), autobiography (Richard Wright's *Black Boy*), novelistic nonfiction (Tracy Kidder's *Among Schoolchildren*), and essay (Gilbert Highet's *The Art of Teaching*).

Conversely, the study of Education assists literary studies by:

◆ Appraising the treatment of educational ideas and experiences in the works of authors as diverse as Joyce, Lawrence, Malamud, and Dickens.

◆ Examining the theme of education itself, whether as schooling or inner growth, in the genre of the *Bildungsroman*, where novels deal with the early development or spiritual education of the lead character.

◆ Assessing such subgenres as the British private school story (Rudyard Kipling's *Stalky and Co.*, Alec Waugh's *The Loom of Youth*), and the campus novel (Kingsley Amis's *Lucky Jim*, Mary McCarthy's *The Groves of Academe*).

◆ Tracing a writer's own educational experience as a source for his work and as evidence of prevailing educational ideas and practices.

I believe that the study of literature has been neglected too long in schools of education. No other subject expresses more fully the "human" in Education considered as one of the *humanities*.

October 1990

35

The Dean's Letter of Personal Agenda (9/19/90)

That was a splendid letter you wrote to the faculty—sympathetic, sensitive, conciliatory. You invite replies. I doubt you will get many. But I suggest you write a summary of what you receive and distribute it to the faculty.

You mention the wide range of faculty views and the need to consider all of them. As I said in my last letter, the more the Graduate School of Education specializes, the more views it generates, and the harder it is to bring people together for the common good. I say again: the GSE is overspecialized, and courses need to be consolidated.

You want to enroll more students of Stanford and Ivy League caliber. What attracts serious students to these and other "elite" universities is the opportunity for scholarly achievement in traditional disciplines. How will they be lured to a GSE that has only one philosopher, one historian, one anthropologist, and no one in literature? If, as you say, UCLA's GSE is *primus inter pares,* that tells you how intellectually provincial those *pares* are. We are not yet among the *academically* elite.

To enroll the best students, the faculty will have to do some recruiting themselves. Another way is to offer a prestige program at the undergraduate level in the discipline of Education, a program as intellectually rigorous and stimulating as competing undergraduate programs. I keep pressing this pro-

69

posal because the present program is oriented, not to Education, but to teaching and schooling, and it is unlikely to attract students who are not now interested in teaching but who could be converted. By contrast, the benefits of my published program, "Education as a Discipline," are on record for all to see. The standard objection to it— lack of resources—ducks the issues I raise.

To find out how faculty are teaching, you will have to attend classes. And faculty should invite colleagues to appraise them. Some of my seminars drew faculty from other departments and schools as well as the GSE. We formed a real community of scholars, and we soon discovered who the challenging teachers were. I knew who the best ones were because I heard them lecture to my classes. I also made it my job to find out what others were up to. So...encourage your people to get together, exchange ideas, share experiences, learn from one another, as you say you want them to.

Your final statement on colleagueship (I prefer collegiality) was well taken. If members of the GSE were more professional and more of an academic community, there would be less need for an emeritus to "meddle" in their affairs. Faculty need to do a good deal more than crank out research papers. Their net worth should be assessed on all that it means to be a professor in a great university. The "all" should be clearly defined and agreed on.

Our faculty should be grateful for your letter of AGENDA. It exemplifies the collegiality you call for. Bear in mind, however, that a leader must be more than a referee. Think how you would like your stewardship to be remembered and act accordingly.

October 1990

36
Why No Endowed Chair in Ed Psych?—1

ecause the subject does not deserve one. Educational psychology is not a cumulative science but a chaos of conflicting theories with no agreed-on tests to decide among them. Its generalizations are equally unreliable, being a collection of tendency statements whose *ceteris paribus* clauses have never been completed.

Most studies in ed psych are trivial, pseudoscientific, and based on dubious assumptions. They are of little use to scholars or teachers. The history of ed psych is a trail of discredited theories. No wonder this history is not taught in this School. The experience would be shattering.

Waving the banner of "science" and appealing to a national pathology (that psychotherapy solves all problems), ed psychs have so hoodwinked the educational establishment that only an intellectual revolution will dislodge them. They have filled our schools of education with behaviorist and cognitivist scientism. They have spawned such delusions as "discovery learning," "reinforcement schedules," "learning as changed behavior," "mediation theory," "transfer of training," "attribution styles," "negative attention-getting," and (so help me) "afferent receptor impulses." How can any intelligent person take this for anything but fashionable claptrap?

In this GSE ed psych never has been taught as a coherent

discipline. In 1953, when I joined this Faculty, Ed Psych 210 was listed as an introduction to the subject as a whole. Some introduction! The professor, an excellent lecturer, taught the learning theories of Watson and Thorndike as if they settled everything. In successive years, he substituted Hull's quirky stimulus–response formulas and then the equally short-lived theories of Guthrie, Gates, Stephens, Tolman, and Spence, followed by a decade of genuflection before the simplicities of Fred Skinner and a half-century in the black hole of behaviorism. The professor finally had the sense to pack it in, his operant response extinct. Asked why he never taught ed psych in the round, he replied, "Who could teach it?"

Instead of compressing their subject, ed psychs have inflated it from a dozen courses in the 1950s to over four dozen today, with little new knowledge to offer to the same number of students as before. Today the GSE is stacked with psychologists, as though Education and ed psych were equivalent. Yet there is no evidence that this monopoly has done anything of consequence for education. The GSE *Development News*, September, 1990, published a summary of some ed psych studies under way. Why not a summary of the effects on K-12 schooling of the studies already completed? It shouldn't take long.

November 1990

37

Why No Endowed Chair in Ed Pysch?—II

Thomas Kuhn called the social sciences at present "immature." He was too charitable. They are permanently immature. Ed psych, for instance, is at a dead end. It has produced no agreed-on theory of teaching, learning, or any other significant educational process.

Cognitive science, now riding to the rescue, treats the mind as software run on the hardware of the brain. It uses the computer as a model of mental processes. Unfortunately most of these processes, such as creativity, resist even the most determined programming efforts. Not even skills, it seems, are learned by applying rules (as the computer applies algorithms) but rather by trial and error, with the rules cooked up later. Anyone who thinks that cognitive science has much to tell education should see...well...a philosopher.

Cognitive science is another of ed psych's lost causes, as Jerome Bruner tells us in his *Acts of Meaning* (Harvard, 1990), while even Howard Gardner hopes for a "brighter postcognitivist future."

In this School of Education the word for all occasions is "exciting." Everyone hails the "exciting" things that happen here. So let's lay on some real intellectual excitement, and save a bundle at the same time. Here's how. Replace a dozen ed psychs with half a dozen philosophers and watch what happens! Our GSE will skyrocket out of range of any other

GSE in the country. Just think! More knowledge for less money. Wouldn't that be "exciting"? The Regents would be ecstatic.

Ed psychs may reply that my criticisms apply equally to philosophy. Not so. Unlike the discredited theories of ed psych, great works of philosophy remain permanently valuable. Philosophy is more self-critical than ed psych. It reflects rigorously on the whole of education, indeed on the entire span of thought. Does ed psych think as rigorously or as well? Philosophers are not so pretentious as to call their work "scientific."

Ed psych should be seen for what it is—the most expensive and expendable specialty on any campus. It should be shaken up and stripped down. True, a few ed psychs have criticized their subject (Cronbach is one). And a few, like Vygotski, Piaget, and Kohlberg, have proposed interesting midlevel theories. Yet none of these theories has been widely accepted, and all rely heavily on philosophy.

In ed psych there is one bright light: Special Education (of disabled children), which is linked to neuropsychiatry. And, yes, some of my best friends are ed psychs. Nevertheless, ed psych would be a poor investment. It already has squandered an unconscionable amount of money. As J. D. Salinger's Holden Caulfield might have said, "It's time to cut this crap." Why don't we?

November 1990

38

Founvations of Education: Not for Teachers Only!

ne reason for the decline in the study of foundations of education is their perversion into how-to courses. A foundations course should be almost entirely theoretical. It should focus on educational ideas, ideals, and accomplishments. It is not a course in the fundamentals of teaching. Its purpose is not to make better teachers, and we should not promise that it will.

Courses in educational foundations may be compared with courses in sociology, which are not designed to produce social workers; or courses in economics, executives; or courses in political science, politicians. To be sure, such courses touch on certain details of social work, business management, and politics, but they do so to illustrate generalizations rather than teach skills. Courses in foundations should do the same. They should present solutions to problems in teaching and schooling as practical applications of educational knowledge, not as models for training.

Students may enroll in foundations courses even if they do not intend to teach. As future parents, voters, and community leaders, they may want to acquire the knowledge basic to informed decisions on educational issues. They should be encouraged to sign up. If the best ones decide to become teachers, they'll be welcome indeed.

George F. Kneller

Some educationists hold that foundations should focus on the problems and practicalities of schooling. They should draw on the "on–going experience of practicing educators." If you define, structure, and classify this information, they claim, you will have the true rationale for foundations of education.

What's wrong with this approach? Just about everything. One, it ignores the formal, background knowledge needed to put this information into perspective. Two, it overlooks the historical, philosophic, and other ideas that have molded education to its present form. Three, it duplicates existing courses in the practical problems of schooling. Four, it dismisses the student with no vocational interest in education, and no taste for the nuts and bolts of practical schooling.

Students should take foundations courses for their contribution to the lives they expect to lead, not as introductions to teaching.

November 1990

39

Evaluation:
Promises, Promises!

ur Evaluation Center has just received a grant for $14.3 million. Hats off to the Center for beating the competition! UCLA gets a cut, and indigent students get to eat better. But is the grant justified? This quantum of cash would pay for a much-needed elementary school, and it would last a hundred years.

Our Evaluation caper began twenty-five years ago, and largesse has poured in ever since. Factored for inflation, asset appreciation, dividend income, and compound interest, the sum accumulated to date, prudently invested and with modest matching funds, would build a brand-new education building, complete with a computer and fax in every office and a plush faculty lounge, serving free coffee and cookies.

Five years ago, Deputy Education Secretary Chester Finn, awarding the Center yet another grant, declared : "We will bust our behinds...to improve the linkage between research and practice" (LA *Times*, November 28, 1985). Where's the improvement, Chester? Give us the evidence!

Five years ago, too, the Center's Director promised (*ibid.*) to "work closely with LA's schools...to apply the Center's more effective, efficient, and fair methods of testing to the classroom." How "effective," "efficient," and "fair" have these methods been? Let's ask Harry Handler to get us an assessment from the LA School Board. If the reply is unfavorable, the bal-

77

ance of the present grant should be returned.

The Director now declares, "We may just have a chance to make assessment work the way we always hoped it would." So, after twenty-five years and umpteen millions, assessment has not worked as expected. What "chance" is there it will "work" in the future?

The Director boasts, "We want to expand the range of legitimate outcomes from schooling well beyond the basics." This grand resolve assumes (a) that the Center has the smarts to define "legitimate outcomes," and (b) that the basics, properly taught, exclude "thinking, problem solving, and developing a sense of competence." That the Center will also "provide more accurate and powerful indicators for public policy" beggars belief, given its failure to "make assessment work" at all. Note the brash, high-flying phraseology, which grantors eat like manna.

The Center swarms with personnel. One must admire its entrepreneurial skill. But how much paper must be shuffled to manage the affairs of its scattered legion? How much energy will be left to study the subject for which the grant was made? What happens to the day to day work of the Graduate School of Education? The commitment to the University? The obligation to students?

January 1991

40

These Missives: A Grant-Free "Evaluation"

Since this is my fortieth *Missive,* an "assessment" is in order. Aside from the occasional "I do not always agree with you," I have yet to receive a serious refutation of any *Missive.* Here are some responses:

• A UC Regent: "I hear your *Missives* are stirring things up down there. That's good. Send me your latest."

• A UC President: "You not only teach philosophy of education, you do it. Congratulations, and keep it up!"

• A UCLA Chancellor: "A splendid piece—clear, bold, and convincing. May I have several copies?"

• A Graduate School of Education Dean: "Your latest *Missive* was a delight...useful, succinct, and humorous. Let's chat about it."

• A GSE Associate Dean: "Your insight is amazing. I now know why your students learn to think."

• A GSE Chairman: "Though they may not say so openly, most of your colleagues are grateful for the knowledge your *Missives* convey."

- **Chairman, Anthropology Department**: "You explain, in most gracious terms, the contribution of anthropology to education. Count on our cooperation."

- **An Area Head**: "In your incomparable fashion you put your finger on some of our most salient research problems."

- **A Senior Colleague**: "Right on! Your courage is an inspiration. How brilliantly you expose *The Leisure of the Theory Class*."

- **A Junior Colleague**: "Your *Missives* light up Moore Hall."

- **An Alumnus**: "Delicious and delightful."

- **Ed Psych Cartel**: "We are not amused."

- **Hearsay**: "He's meddling in our affairs! He's trying to run the place!! Do what he says and we'll have nothing to teach!!!" (Good points, all of them.)

- *School and Society*: "We are pleased to publish your *Missive*, 'True Breadth.' It's a gem. Any more like it?"

February 1991

41

Diversity, Multiculturalism, and the Future of the GSE

iversity and multiculturalism are the insistent pieties of our time. On diversity, Vice Chancellor Paredes declares that certain "margins" of the curriculum should move to the "center." On multiculturalism, UC Berkeley Chancellor Tien predicts that in a decade or so "there will be no majority population ...and we shall have to educate in terms of a multicultural society." How will UCLA's Graduate School of Education respond to these challenges? What meaning do they have for schools of education everywhere?

Since it's agreed that the University should be fair, every culture will be included in the curriculum. Chicano studies, for instance, will be joined by the Hispanic (Mexican, Cuban, Puerto Rican, Latin American). Since we have African–American and Asian–American studies, room will be made for Euro–American studies, Arab–American, Indian–American, etc. And since this nation embraces every culture, all will be represented in some form.

Equal treatment of ethnic groups will spawn specialties *ad infinitum.* It also will generate classification problems. Should Philippino-Americans take Asian or Latin American studies? How many types of Slavic-American studies should there be? Russian, Polish, Czech, Ukrainian, Serb, *et al?* Among Asian-Americans, how many types? Japanese–American, Chinese,

Korean, Vietnamese, *et al.* Where will Armenians and Iranians fit?

What's in store for our current educational disciplines (history, philosophy, psychology, etc.)? They will vanish into the new ethnospecialties. Their FTEs will be distributed among Chicano ed psych, Hispanic ed soash, Arab ed history, African ed phil, Indian ed anthro, and so on. The tree of Moore Hall will branch into a thousand twigs!

Who will teach these new curricular exotica? Sterner pietists say, like should teach like. That means African teachers for African students, Latinos for Latinos, Arabs for Arabs, and so on. This ethnic cleansing allegedly will promote both personal and cultural self-esteem, psychological as well as intellectual growth. The GSE will glow like a rainbow.

Since the GSE will be enhancing its regard for other cultures, the faculty will need to read, study, and teach in an array of languages. Señor Paredes wants us to study more languages, and as a polyglot I heartily agree with him. Yet most faculty are monolingual, monocultural. It seems they will have to diversify, get multicultural, multilingual...or perish. Better start now!

Will diversity/multiculturalism promote unity or division? Cultural cohesion or cultural conflict? Only research, lots of it, will tell. But common sense suggests that opposites will not always attract, and that multiculturalism could end up in a gridlock.

How to fund this new Enlightenment? Elect the right politicians!

QUOT CULTURAE, TOT SENTENTIAE!

March 1991

42

James W. Guthrie: "Educational Research and Politics"

im Guthrie is a University of California Berkeley educational psychologist whose learning theories once were a feature of Educational Psychology 212. So his article, "Educational Research and Politics" (*Ed Researcher,* March 1990), is worth noting, though it is poorly argued and based on a false premise. I discuss this piece because: (a) Guthrie is one of the best ed psychs in the country; (b) he makes the same mistakes as do other education researchers; and (c) he knows ed psych history but hasn't learned from it.

Guthrie calls educational research "ineffectual." I agree. It is dismissed by educators and politicians alike, because it produces few financial, political, or even educational benefits. It is whipped up by education professors desperate to reconcile two incompatible ends: to please referees and promotion committees on the one hand and help schools on the other.

Guthrie focusses on nuts and bolts research into problems of schooling. He assumes that this alone is ed research, and this alone advances the discipline of Education. Thus he reinforces the bias of education professors in general, who doubt that Education will ever make it as an academic discipline, yet, to win promotion, state their findings in disciplinary terms. In my view, this is another reason ed research is "ineffectual."

Jim also claims that education research is "inadequate" be-

83

cause it gets less money than medical research. Yet some projects are awash in cash (like our twenty–five–year-old Evaluation caper). What he should have said, and documented, is that much well–funded education research has produced inadequate results—inadequate because it consists of minor variations on outdated, quasi-scientific paradigms.

Jim then asserts that medical research has more, and more powerful, supporters than education research. The former, he says, include physicians (though less numerous than educators), pharmaceutical and biotechnical industries (though eclipsed by the makers of education products), hospitals and convalescent homes (though fewer than education institutions), and public health officials (though vastly outnumbered by education administrators). Guthrie to the contrary, the power base for education research is immense. It simply awaits better research proposals than those produced thus far.

Guthrie rightly points out that education practitioners are "actively estranged" from schools of education. They avoid professors of education, claiming that their work is "irrelevant."

What is Guthrie's remedy for this state of affairs? An indigestible stew of five ingredients: popular, philosophic, professional, political, pragmatic (his terms). What is my prescription? A good dose of conceptual analysis and a high regard for the economics of scarce resources.

One final question: Why did Guthrie exclude the psychological from these ingredients? Had he perhaps read my *Missives* on the futility of ed psych?

April 1991

43

"Poca Ricerca, Molta Produzione!"

ascinated by my *Missive 41*, "Diversity, Multiculturalism, and the Future of the GSE," Mrs. Enrico Manzoni, head of the Manzoni Foundation, had me to lunch some time ago to find out how the Foundation could help the Graduate School of Education reach the goals I had proposed, such as saving the curriculum from cultural radicals. There was no need to apply for a grant, she said, such applications were "*camuffamento*" anyway. After lunch she handed me a generous check to the University. When I promised to finish the project in less than a week, she shook her head: "*Impossibile...incredibile...mai nello passato!*"

The Manzonis came from Italy with no English, little money, poor job prospects, and faced discrimination. Signore Manzoni, a plumber, worked nights and weekends on emergency calls and Signora Manzoni waited on tables. They learned English on the job. Enrico soon formed his own plumbing company and his wife bought the restaurant where she worked. The Manzoni Foundation is now the charitable arm of Manzoni Industries.

I went to work at once. First I examined every possible form of research. I reviewed research design, survey data analysis, and evaluation theory. That took half an hour. Analyzing the concepts involved in the project took several hours... and into the next day. I then spent another half hour on analysis of variance (since I was studying diversity) and multivariates (for multiculturalism). But I found no real difference between survey research and poll-taking, despite claims that the former is said to be more sophisticated. So I settled on a survey.

During the next few days I interviewed a "sample" of the GSE faculty. That was some task! Where were my colleagues? Some seemed permanently "in class," though they taught only one or two classes a week. Many were "out of town" at meetings. I did hit on a committee for "Teacher Evaluation in an Age of Transition," whose members couldn't agree when the transition began or when it would end. Two students, waiting to see their professors, were squat on a mattress they had brought. A class in Moore Hall dismissed itself after ten minutes because the teacher failed to show up. Still, I persevered.

On the sixth and final day I typed my findings on a single page (as usual) and delivered it to the Manzonis. I also returned their check, suggesting that they spend their money on the education of disabled children. The Manzonis were ecstatic. "*Poca ricerca,*" cried Enrico, "*molta produzione!*" The next day he had copies made and sent to every institution of higher education in the country. Later I saw Mrs. Manzoni place the original page in her family Bible. "*Precioso,*" she said.

Last week the Manzoni Foundation awarded UCLA $14.3 million, stipulating that the income from it be used in perpetuity by the GSE and the Med School Neuropsychiatric Institute for Disabled Children.

April 1991

44

In Praise of Elites

ew words are abused more than "elite." Coming from the Latin *eligere*, to choose, via the French *élite*, it means, according to Webster's dictionary, "a choice part or segment, as of a social, political, or professional group."

In common speech, however, notably among leftists, "elite" is a term of contempt for snobs and blue bloods—members of old-boy networks who acquire power through social or family connections, own more property and exercise more influence than they should, and at their worst are fascists and advocates of eugenics.

Opponents of elitism tend to be distrustful of authority (which they confuse with authoritarianism) and suspicious of leadership. They are wedded to equality in everything and dedicated to the cause of the average man (whoever he may be). Down with rank! Out with social distinction! Let's all muck in together! How ironic, then, that university professors, when up for promotion, assert that they are leaders in their fields.

Today many anti–elitists are giving the kiss of life to selected doctrines of old–time "progressive education." In the name of equality and social reconstruction they oppose classroom prizes, citations for special achievement, grade retention, and accelerated promotion. Teachers and students must forge a "new" and "just" society, bringing down the plutocrats and "empowering the dispossessed." Despite the manifest, largely unalterable inequality of actual human beings, these levelers denounce tests of intelligence, aptitude, and ability, calling them insensitive, discriminatory, and anti-democratic.

It's time to dispel this warped attitude. The true elite are not "privileged," but people of rare talent who have greatly benefited the human race. It is self-evident that all scientific and philosophic advances, all achievements in music, art, literature, and technology have been the work of innovators from every social sphere. Elites, said William James, are our "proudest products" or, as the French say, *la fleur de la patrie* (the flower of the nation).

In universities especially, we must work harder to produce intellectual and professional elites whom our rivals will never equal. Who will be the first to offer studies in elitism? What a peak educational experience that would be!

August 1991

45

Ed Psych: A Response and My Rejoinder

finally received a formal reply to two *Missives*, both on ed psych, from a senior professor of the subject at a major university. Here is the gist of his letter and my rejoinder.

You are right to ask why I call ed psych "pretentious" yet claim that philosophy "covers all disciplines." My comments on the matter were too brief. I should have said that philosophers reflect on the most fundamental concepts used in, and the most general questions presupposed by, the different disciplines. This is a necessary task of thought, and not in the least pretentious. What is the pretense, for example, when philosophers examine the conceptual foundations of, and the empirical evidence for, behaviorism, psychoanalysis, cognitivism, and other schools of psychology? They are simply doing their job.

Any impartial observer who contrasts the long history, broad scope, and rigorous standards of philosophy with the endemic shortcomings of psychology surely will agree that ed psych is absurdly overrepresented and philosophy shamefully under-represented in schools of education. Who can contemplate the squabbling sects and the absence of agreed-on findings in an endeavor that calls itself an empirical science, and not deplore the inflated reputation of this discipline and the gross neglect of the other? That is why I call ed psych "pretentious."

One cause of philosophy's neglect is the refusal of its adherents to match the strident claims made by the hucksters for ed psych. Most philosophers don't know how to talk to the rank and file faculty. They are reluctant salesmen, less inclined than ed psychs to pitch promises and raise hopes.

You state: "Only three theoretical positions underlie work in ed psych: situationism, trait or individual difference orientation, and interactionism...and...there is a growing consensus around the interactive model as the prevalent theoretical approach." These "positions," as you describe them, sound more like concepts for classifying theories than theoretical frameworks ("positions") to which theories of psychology can be reduced. For example, if each of a dozen theories posits an interaction between variables, you have a dozen different theories of an interactional type, not a dozen versions of a single theory. But why do you ignore the major psychological research traditions, some of which I mentioned earlier?

I agree that learning can enhance intelligence, and "one can never learn less from any experience," but what is one learning? The more untruths you learn, the more deluded you get. If you learn from one field only, you become monomaniac. Talk to a flat earther and see whether his study has enhanced his intelligence. "Learning" and "intelligence" are terms to be handled with care.

I admit I don't read as much ed psych as ed psychs would like. The reason is that most of it does not enhance the intelligence, and life is too short to waste it on such deadening pedantry.

Thanks anyhow for writing me. You may be consoled by Cicero's observation, "There is nothing so absurd but some philosopher has said it."

August 1991

46

What is Education?
A Letter to an Indian Educationist

Some time ago the Head of the Education Department at Allahabad University, India, asked me: "What do we study when we study education? What should be our goals? Is education a science or a humanity? What methods should it use? How does it progress?" He had read widely but found no satisfying answers. Here is the gist of my reply.

When we study education we examine the ideas, artifacts, and events involved in teaching, learning, schooling, administering, enculturing, etc. We study these phenomena directly and also through the lenses of the humanities and the human sciences.

As a study, the goals of education are: (a) to understand the ideas, practices, and possibilities of the educational process; (b) to improve teaching, learning, and schooling; (c) to train educationists and educators; and (d) to help parents and citizens vote intelligently on educational issues and contribute to the educational process at all levels.

There is little science but much scientism in the study of education. The educational process can rarely be controlled, measured, or predicted. Hence few generalizations are universal and few findings are replicable. As a humanity, education uses common sense, imagination, and broad knowledge to interpret events and texts, as well as to create and appraise

91

theories and improve practice. Education usually reflects the values and personal commitments of the scholar, just as the educational process reflects those of the teacher.

The study of education uses many methods. The history of education employs narrative and documentary analysis. The philosophy of education analyzes concepts and deploys and examines arguments. Literary studies apply critical techniques to poetry, the novel, the essay, and the memoir as they relate to education. As a human science, education prefers empirical approaches. Educational anthropology, for instance, relies mainly on participant observation. Administrative studies use operations analysis, statistical analysis, and accounting techniques.

In order to progress, education must become an independent discipline, able to conduct research in all areas of educational thought and practice. The different fields must be linked by common concepts and principles, by interdisciplinary studies (*e.g.*, social history, cultural studies, cognitive science, literary-legal studies, and political economy), by philosophic analysis, and above all by a master theory of education in all its aspects. A discipline of this kind will remove the chief obstacles to progress in educational studies: fragmentation, incoherence, and lack of focus.

Because attitudes toward education vary from person to person and culture to culture, education must be a humanity rather than a science. To achieve greater educational unity throughout the world, more attention must be paid to comparative and international education, sadly underestimated by most educationists in this country.

Summer 1991

47

For the GSE: A Route to Excellence

For as long as I can remember, people have disagreed on what this School of Education should do to achieve excellence. There has been talk recently of defining the "mission" of the GSE, but no definition has emerged or seems likely to. So let me propose some steps that I think will lead to the status we all desire.

◆ Find out what interests and visions faculty and students have in common. Invite alumni to state what they believe to be the GSE's unique quality or the quality the GSE should cultivate.

◆ Be concerned about student-faculty relations. For instance, ask faculty and students what these relations are now, what they have been, and what they can be in the future. Study particular relations in depth with a view toward recreating them.

◆ Raise the level of teaching by appointing more faculty of known teaching ability, by inviting star teachers as guest lecturers, by encouraging faculty to attend and learn from one another's classes, and by rewarding teaching ability more substantially.

◆ Increase intellectual attainment by holding special sessions, open to the public, in which faculty discuss their current or future projects, by encouraging faculty to attend campus-wide seminars, by inviting more guest lecturers, and by publicly citing outstanding research.

◆ Publicize the vital contributions of research to the theory and practice of higher education and the solution of problems throughout the teaching profession.

◆ Integrate the GSE by reducing the five current Divisions to two—one academic, the other professional—and encouraging these two to cooperate. This change would not affect specialized studies, except by clarifying their relevance to education as a whole. The GSE should assume that, notwithstanding its diversity, the discipline of Education has a basic structure. This School should endorse Alfred North Whitehead's "seamless web" conception of knowledge.

◆ Cooperate more closely with related departments on campus. In particular, see that the GSE is represented on every campus committee devoted to educational development, thus giving the School a greater voice in University affairs.

If the GSE acts on these suggestions, it will be distinguished by enviable student-faculty relations, a unified faculty, an interdisciplinary emphasis, a model program of demonstratcd cxcellence in teaching, and research of both intellectual and practical importance. Excellence will not be achieved, however, unless individual faculty members are willing to serve the School as a whole. As the School transforms itself, so will they.

Summer 1991

94

48

"On the Street by 93-94"

n August 29, 1991, Stanford's Professor Michael Kirst and Federal Research Director Milton Goldberg testified before an education subcommittee of state governors on the creation of a national assessment program.

Some testimony! When asked what research so far had been delivered to justify the millions spent on it, they ducked the question. When reminded of President Bush's "93-94 on the Street" deadline for definitive action, they waffled. They would try to meet the challenge but could do a better job if the date were more flexible. When have we heard that before?

Goldberg hailed UCLA's Evaluation Center for its decision to "establish" procedures (rather than merely talk about them). Asked what had been established so far, Goldberg spoke only of "possible outcomes." But here at UCLA the "outcomes" have remained "possible" for decades (*Missive* 39: "Evaluation").

The governors listened politely but soon grew impatient. More than one cited the persistent failure of research to improve the nation's schools. The witnesses conceded this had been so in the past, but claimed that "some progress" was now being made in "some (unnamed) schools." Do these include the schools of Los Angeles, the immediate beneficiaries of the UCLA colossus? Can Harry Handler give the governors some figures? I doubt it.

The governors then brought up some issues the witnesses themselves should have addressed. Other nations, they said, seem to be educating better than us, so what can we learn from them? The witnesses granted the point but made no suggestions. Yes, some corporations were successful in screening potential employees, but schools could not learn from them without doing "a lot of research." Yes, it's true that some schools with similar teachers, similar students, in similar communities were doing much better than others. Why? That was a "mystery." I swear it, that was their reply. That alone reveals how genuinely naive our educational leaders are and exposes the true payoff we can expect from research.

I now predict that President Bush's call for action will stimulate an immense outflow of "scholarship," truckloads of paper stacked with statistics and fattened with footnotes, warning that findings are "inconclusive" and "more research is needed."

I repeat (*Missive* 27): (1) One sure way to improve our schools is to raise the standard of teaching substantially and enlist the help of capable parents and lay people. (2) The only "additional funds" needed for this are generous scholarships to attract the finest people to teaching. (3) The best way to boost the performance of teachers in service is to reward them handsomely for achievement, making the profession genuinely meritocratic. To accomplish all this, we do not need more research but more imagination, common sense, and self–criticism.

September 1991

49

GSEs: Who Needs Them?

This is a wake–up call. Of the 20,000 plus professors of education in this country only a handful sit on blue-ribbon committees for educational reform. It is painfully obvious that educationists everywhere are rejected in favor of people who may never have studied education at all. No profession is as marginal as ours.

What has this Graduate School of Education done for policy and practice, even at UCLA? How often do colleagues in other fields look to us for educational leadership? Instead of producing new ideas or adding to our fund of genuine knowledge, most faculty accumulate microscopic "findings" to fatten their bios.

Our Dean recently asked the faculty how teaching and research should be evaluated. How many of them responded? None. What did our evaluation "experts" say? Nothing. So here's my advice. When a teacher is up for promotion, ask:

◆ How do you define successful teaching?

◆ What educational theory does this definition presuppose?

◆ Mention one case where you failed as a teacher and tell why.

◆ Say how others rate you as a teacher. Comment on their assessments.

As for researchers, ask:

◆ How would you contrast educational research with other types?

◆ What are your research goals?

◆ What educational theory are your findings based on?

◆ What have you shown that was not known or thought of before?

Do not be annoyed by these questions. They go to the heart of your professional life. They reflect what you say you are teaching.

Why is educational research so ineffective? Partly because it fails to produce findings and recommendations that are challenging, relevant, and practical. But mostly because there is no fully realized discipline of Education to guide research in any field. Without this disciplinary frame GSEs everywhere have become loose aggregates of arcane specialisms with no shared foundations, no common mission, no roots from which true professionalism can grow. Topics replace courses, specialized studies are spun off, and the whole show is in free fall.

Our faculty must stop thinking and acting like the *apparatchiki* of a Rand Corporation. Most current research is trivial or pointless. It could be done by intelligent students. If you doubt this, look at some issues of the *Daily Bruin*.

September 1991

50

If Parkinson and Peter Can. . . .

n any intellectual endeavor originality is proportional to knowledge of history.

◆ The more an organization innovates, the more its new ideas fail.

◆ Work tends to increase in proportion to the number of machines available to do it.

◆ The more a teacher admires a student, the more she sees someone like herself.

◆ In any educational system individual freedom varies inversely as community demands are satisfied.

◆ The validity of an intelligence test varies with its power to tell parents how bright their children are.

◆ The more you believe in flexibility, the less you obey the Ten Commandments.

◆ A theory of change is true for as long as the moment of its conception.

◆ The more you strive for originality, the less you cite your sources.

◆ The reaction of any system to external stimuli is proportional to the frequency of input (typical psychobabble).

◆ The more you study history, the more you realize the future isn't what it was.

◆ The more you treat people as equals, the less important you yourself become.

◆ The more the truth hurts, the more lies you tell.

◆ The more you reach for a place in the sun, the hotter life gets.

◆ The more you read stuff like this, the nuttier you become.

September 1991

51

"Strategic Plan, May 1991": From a GSE to a Training College

This is a wretched report. It appears to be the work of three people, whose thinking it clearly reflects. Three other signatories seem to have just been present. The remaining three disappeared without a trace. The report is written in unrelieved "edspeak." Remove the repetition and redundancy and the present ten pages would drop to seven. Cut the *nonsequiturs* and the "fadthink," and you're left with four. In fact, I could put the lot on one page and save the reader from boredom.

Plowing through this waste requires a high tolerance for buzzwords, like "structures," "goals," "practices," "models," "directions," "strategies." We are told repeatedly of "changes": "vast...unprecedented...demanding...and difficult changes." My O my! And of "progress," which (so help me!) the Graduate School of Education must "monitor...improve...and (naturally) evaluate." We are going to be very busy indeed.

Yes, it's only a plan, and the faculty are asked to fill in the blanks. But don't be deceived. The blanks aren't there for university education. If the "planners" have their way, the GSE no longer will exist. What we have here, when the blanks are filled in, is a Graduate School of Practical Schooling. For the plan appeals to no theory. It is committed solely to the "practical," and even that is undefined and undefended.

The Dean asked for a plan on academic programs. There

is nothing academic here, nothing on subject matter, scholarship, creative teaching/learning—only a trudge through the
"practical." And I mean trudge. There are no arguments, no at-
tempts to justify or persuade, just one long promenade of as-
sertions.

The outline format is deceptive. It gives the impression
that here is something tightly structured. But the structure is a
house of cards, ready to collapse under a breath of fresh air.
The elaborate section heads and paragraph leads, turned out
in different fonts, introduce nothing but verbiage.

A few good ideas peek through the murk. The plan calls
for more "community." It urges faculty to become more involved with our Teacher Education Laboratory. It recommends
greater collaboration among the divisions. It also announces
that "the divisions present arguments for breadth" but adds
ambivalently that they "support relatively discrete foci" (whatever that means). It proposes "indicators" (a hurrah word) to
measure progress, but, I fear, all are quantitative. They ask,
"How many times?"

This report is pedantic to the end. "The GSE," it perorates,
"should not delay in enunciating its own goals and strategies
and in developing ways to gather feedback [gawd!] to determine the efficacy of its practices." Read this "conclusion" first
and deep–six the rest.

October 1991

102

52

What's All This about "Rich Subject Matter"? Philosophy, Psychology, and Merl Wittrock

Twenty years ago, in a review of *Learning Theories* by psychologists Pittenger and Gooding (*Educational Forum*, November 1972), Merl C. Wittrock alerted learning theorists to "the rich subject matter" of philosophy. He hailed the book as a "first approximation toward an analysis in depth of the relation of the two subjects." The connection, he insisted, is "fundamentally important in education.... We can learn more about education by relating psychology and philosophy to each other."

Right on Merl! But how much have ed psychs "related" their subject to philosophy lately? How much have you? If the relation is so "important," why are you silent when the Graduate School of Education supports twenty ed psychs for one philosopher? When does the "in-depth analysis" begin? Since you do not tell us how the subjects are related, let me help.

Philosophers explore such psychological constructs as personality, self, human nature and behavior, mind-body relations, motivation, and practically everything listed in the indexes of ed psych textbooks. They work on conceptual problems and the general questions presupposed by ed psych research. They propose theories that frame or conceptualize a field—Locke's for William James, Kant's for Piaget and Kohlberg, Nelson Goodman's for Bruner. They also submit theories of their own that often are empirically testable, *e.g.*,

Dennett's and Fodor's in cognitive science, Harré's in social psychology, and those of Komisar, Macmillan, Ennis, and McPeck in the psychology of critical thinking. Philosophers also propose and analyze premises for psychological theories: Quine and the logical empiricists for behaviorism, Peters and Taylor against; the Churchlands for cognitive science, Searle and Dreyfus against.

Philosophers assess the rationality of the knowledge claims and procedures of psychology. Chomsky, for instance, destroys Skinner, Grünbaum demolishes Freud, Scriven evaluates evaluation, and D. C. Phillips and David Ericson critique the methods and conclusions of ed psych research.

Philosophy and psychology often interact, attacking the same topics and sometimes using similar methods. Psychologists Bruner and Kagan scan the philosophic foundations of psychology. Cronbach discusses the nature of psychological laws. Philosophers Hampshire, Goldman, Flanagan, and those in cognitive science draw conclusions from select psychological "findings," which otherwise may be unusable or not well-confirmed.

If ed psychs want to get anywhere, they must lean on philosophy every step of the way. So, Merl, have the courage of your convictions. Act as though that "relation" existed. Stump for more philosophers in the GSE.

For very few ed psychs know what philosophers are talking about. It is arcane chatter to them. Small wonder that so much of their work is fruitless.

Fall 1991

53

Psychohistory and Its Follies—1

isciplinary mergers work when the disciplines are compatible. Physical chemistry succeeds because the sciences complement each other. So does social psychology. But when disciplines are at odds, one may swallow the other, as physics has with biology in biophysics. Sociobiology has inched forward in such quantified fields as bio- and sociometrics, but elsewhere it remains speculative (*Missive* 25). Cognitive science, in contrast, is a fertile mix of artificial intelligence, cognitive psychology, and the philosophy of mind. Philosophy is the glue that holds this science together.

Psychohistory, however, has no future. In theory psychohistorians use psychoanalysis to solve historical puzzles, *e.g.*, about the motives of historical agents. In practice they surrender to it. In almost every psychohistorical study Freud overpowers Clio. Yet psychoanalysis itself, one of a dozen major psychological schools, is hardly more than a blip in the history of the study of the mind. If psychoanalysis shrinks history, it surely will do the same to the study of education.

What is the purpose of psychohistory? Is it to record facts and ideas? Explore the inner lives of historical agents? Explain the history of psychoanalysis itself? Account for social practices such as education? I am not splitting hairs. To do their job properly, psychohistorians in education will have to master

105

three disciplines, each with its own methods—history, psychoanalysis, and education. A tall order for a tiny specialty.

Psychoanalysis, we are told, is the answer to permissivism. Freud held that civilization depends on the suppression of instinct. For him, enculturation entails the submission of impulse and desire to social and cultural "reality." Learning-as-fun must yield to learning-as-obligation. But what does this general thesis imply for educational practice? Does it mandate stern discipline and student self-denial in the unraveling schools of multiethnic America? Recall that Freud sought to explain the inner lives and symptoms of neurotic patients, not resolve the mundane problems of ordinary schools. Asked about the significance of his work for education, Freud replied that the question "bewildered" him.

Appalled by the excessive permissivism and the emphasis on children's rights without commensurate responsibilities, Anna Freud applied her father's ideas to education. She reminds us that children lack the psychological, ethical, and intellectual development to be treated as mature citizens. Yet her proposals rest on the false promises and faulty conclusions of the psychoanalytic movement as a whole (*Missive* 54).

The study of education calls on so many fields it has been dubbed the "marketplace of ideas." The study of history is even more encompassing. In principle at least it is the narrative of all that has happened. How can psychoanalysis, with its limited agenda, do justice to two such omnivorous disciplines? It is destined to stagger beneath a universe it cannot cope with.

November 1991

54

Psychohistory and Its Follies—II

amed by Isaac Asimov, psychohistory has remained an enclave of the surreal for a quarter century. Its adherents began by dishing out plain old Viennese Freud: drive-reduction, oedipal conflict, incestuous and parricidal wishes, castration fears, repetition compulsion, toilet traumas, you name it. Many still do. For them history was one long psychodrama.

Eventually such reductionism made a few uneasy. After all, if everyone hauls the same demons around, why did Sigmund Freud alone, and not every other little Freud, write an *Interpretation of Dreams*? If all of us are crippled by childhood, how could Einstein revolutionize physics? If infant failures determine us, what influence is exerted by religion, schooling, economics, social class, political institutions, ideologies, and the other engines of historical change?

Some psychohistorians have turned to later developments in analysis (ego psychology, object-relations theory, self psychology). Yet all such schools remain wide open to the standard anti-Freudian critique. Psychoanalysis overflows with anecdotal evidence that can always be explained by one theory or another. What it lacks are data based on confirmed predictions that refute rival theories. It is logically incoherent, empirically unwarranted, and culturally parochial. Moreover, psychoanalysis aims at a cure, for which an analyst's interpretation is

107

acceptable if his patient believes it and gets well, regardless of its truth or falsity. How can such an enterprise aim squarely at truth, the goal of historical inquiry?

Have psychohistorians used conventional psychology? They have. Personal, developmental, and social psychology—specifically social learning theory, trait-factor analysis, and phenomenology—all have been tried. The results? "Surprisingly meager," says one psychohistorian. Surprisingly? What else should be expected from a circus of competing theories, whose findings are either trivial or truistic, or common sense clotted with jargon and statistics? (*Missives 36, 38*)

Princeton historian Laurence Stone calls psychohistory a "disaster area." "Psychoanalysis," he says, "has not been much use to the historian, who is normally unable to penetrate the bedroom, the bathroom, and the nursery. If Freud is right, and these are the places where the action is, there is not much he can do about it."

Yet psychohistorians keep churning the stuff out. And some educationists, against all the evidence, cling to the belief that all this speculation might turn out to be true. I am reminded of astrologers who, impervious to rational or scientific critique, advise us that the stars are out there still, waiting to be interpreted.

November 1991

55

How Spoileᕤ You Are!—1

hen I arrived in 1953, UCLA counted 20,000 students and 1,200 faculty. Today it has 35,000 students and 3,000 faculty. How much has academic performance been fueled by this dramatic improvement in the faculty-student ratio? Let's see.

I came as an associate professor. My salary was $5,000 with no perquisites. The average teaching load was 3+ courses. I was assigned 4+. Today the average load is 2-courses and the equivalent salary is $50,000 plus perquisites. The academic year has been cut 10%.

The School (Department) of Education occupied the first two floors of Moore Hall. The third floor belonged to the Home Economics Department and the UCLA band, whose members were allowed to practice from noon to one but often tooted at will. Today we occupy the whole of Moore Hall and have invaded other halls. Are we better for being bigger?

The School (Department) numbered around 1,200 undergraduate students and 400 graduate students. The faculty taught more students than today. There were no "Divisions," just one highly collegial, highly argumentative group. I argued continually with May Seagoe on the facts of what she called "school psychology" and with Evan Keislar on what he called "instructional psychology." How far has ed psych advanced beyond these constructs?

There was one dean and one associate dean. There was no chairman or chairwoman and chairs were what you sat on. The dean had one secretary, Marge, who ran the place. For anything at all, you asked Marge. She had one assistant, two typists, and a student runner. That was the office force. There was no office of admissions; just one simple, efficient administrative setup, which never closed for lunch.

UCLA had one chancellor and one assistant, each with a highly efficient executive secretary. There were no provosts and few deans. Today we have a galaxy of vice chancellors, associates, assistants, along with their associates and assistants and a retinue of subordinates sitting at computers, copiers, and faxes; we have over a hundred deans—full, associate, and assistant—all with their own retinue of secretaries. Want to promote a dean? Make him a provost! Prime qualification? An ability to straddle. Let's not forget the demimonde: a horde of counselors, advisers, quasi-academics, and yes, assistants and secretaries. Murphy Hall now is twice its old size with twice as many entrances and elevators for its three floors. Ten truckloads of paper roll in and out of UCLA daily.

In 1953 male students wore coats or sweaters and ties. So did teachers. Coeds were neat and trim in gingham dresses. In the rowdy–dowdy 60s all standards of dress and behavior collapsed. Teachers turned on and became hippies (as many still do). I had to take over one class when the teacher lost control. Every day the *Bruin* expectorated passionate articles on sex and pot.

Fall 1991

56

How Spoiled You Are!—II

ntil we became a Graduate School my Foundations classes averaged 500 students. Once there were so many we had to meet in Royce Hall. Since neither Royce nor Moore 100 had sound systems, I had to lecture *voce fortissima*, taking questions in the aisles. Royce had no desks, and the lighting was, shall we say, crepuscular. Unless I electrified my students, they dozed off. I corrected papers into the night and returned them with comment.

A master's degree required a thesis and an exam in French or German (a doctorate, both French and German). I used to prep students for these exams *pro bono*. Theses and dissertations were as dismal then as now.

Research? I did it weekends and vacations. (Too busy during the week teaching, preparing lectures, correcting papers, seeing students.)

Sabbaticals? Only if you got a colleague to teach your classes. So I once taught both ed soc and ed psych. The texts weighed a ton, but I covered them in half a dozen lectures and went on to social and psychological philosophy, from Plato to Marx. The students ate up existential psychology. They couldn't get it anywhere else. Likewise the logic and psychology of curriculum and instruction.

Faculty were more adventurous then. I introduced educational anthropology and set up a "humanistics" seminar attended by faculty from all over the campus. I taught "Principles of Leadership" to UCLA's ROTC cadets (sheer bliss!). Before a full house I debated Art Lumsdaine on instructional technology, also Jim Popham on behavioral objectives. Jim taped the debate and sold a million copies—the one behavioral objective that really paid off for him. I think he slipped me $50. I took on so many contenders the Dean advised me to cool it. Moore Hall ceased to vibrate...for a while.

In the 60s, along with student hotheads, ed psychs infiltrated in force. They soon had enough votes to run the show (as they still do). Also, the Evaluation clique got their first grant. Walls tumbled, floors were torn up, toilets were moved, furniture fetched—all to celebrate what we now call CRESST. I warned the Graduate School of Education it was a boondoggle and time has vindicated me (*Missives 39* and *48*).

The University, once solvent, now lives beyond its means. Have the reforms it has funded produced any real gains? No, according to latest UC reports. Undergraduate education has been allowed to drift. Inept TAs do the teaching. The tenured don't teach enough. Too much research is trite and trivial (*Missives 11* and *72*).

How about education in the GSE? What have *you* done to improve it? Can you point to the difference (*Missive 47*)? You have been spoiled too long. The ax will be wielded throughout the UC system, this GSE included (*Missive 30*).

So the most urgent task awaiting the GSE is to summarize and assess the educational effects of the changes made over the last ten years. The central question to answer is: How much would education suffer if Moore Hall were shut down for good (*Missive 49*)? But don't overreact. Just continue to research those micro–studies that fatten your bios but have no further meaning.

Fall 1991

57

Kudos to My Colleagues

To Jim Popham for his article, "A Slice of Advice," *Ed Researcher*, December, 1991: "Find a colleague who will provide candid reactions to your work; then venerate that colleague...for when it comes to criticizing a co-worker's efforts, most colleagues are wimps. Faced with such wimpiness, it is inordinately difficult to find a colleague whom you can trust to tell you when your shabby efforts are, in truth, shabby...that your most recent 'breakthrough' should be sent to the paper-shredder. I've been gratified during my career to have had two or three such colleagues." On target, Jim!

◆ To Marvin Alkin for his stunning admission in the 1991 NSSE Yearbook: "Most of the writing on evaluation, including my own, seems to be mechanistic and prescriptive, seeming to imply that there are certain specific procedures and protocols to be followed which, if properly done, will lead to a professional and expert evaluation." Marvin regrets that "experts endorse a mode of evaluation which excludes the personal views and insights of the evaluator." You've seen the light, Marv.

◆ To Eva Baker for treating me to a splendid lunch (at the Bel Air). For over two hours we swapped ideas on everything

113

but evaluation, which, for me, at least, would have been a trifle next to the substance of our *tête-a-tête*.

◆ **To Merl Wittrock** for his appointment to a seven-member AERA Committee on Ethics, five of whom are philosophers. Tell us, Merl, what you learned from those thinkers. Explain why the Graduate School of Education needs twenty ed psychs to balance one philosopher. Can we expect a closer "relation" in the near future?

◆ **To Charlotte Crabtree** for bagging a huge grant to write a K-12 history curriculum for the public schools by 1994. Charlotte maintains that history teaching was "dumbed down during the 1970s and early 1980s." We hear you, Charlotte. So her Center for the Teaching of History will develop a curriculum stretching from prehistory to the breakup of the USSR. Let's hope her colleagues can handle it. I fear that too many special interests—ethnic groups with agendas, assorted teachers, parents, and publics—will produce a feeding frenzy. The likely result? A curriculum of compromises and concessions, a "victory" of the margins over the center, Hopi over Hannibal. Yet, whatever the outcome, the project has brought both money and prestige to the GSE. My forecast for 1994? Sunny. For a "revolution in the teaching of history"? Cloudy. Too many troughs ahead.

◆ **To Norma Feshbach**, our interim Dean, for steering us through the turbulent move from Moore to Maxxam. You kept the ship on course with the hatches open. Nice work, Norma!

January 1991

58

The "Unschooled" Gardner

oward Gardner is thoughtful, fluent, and well-read. He has written stylish, challenging syntheses—*hautes vulgarisations* with an original core. So I expected *The Unschooled Mind* (Basic Books, 1991) to be absorbing and plausible. It is neither. It is the Harvard *bricoleur's* least convincing collage.

It runs like this. By age 5-6 the child has developed seven separate intelligences and an "intuitive" understanding of the world. Onto this ferment the school clamps a carapace of formal learning. The two understandings, the intuitive and the schooled, do not mesh. So when a student (or adult) has to solve a new problem, he tends to abandon his school knowledge and fall back on a naive intuition inadequate to the world's more complex demands. To prevent this regression, Gardner urges educators to adopt certain institutions and practices which (he says) will harmonize the two understandings: "apprenticeships," "exploratoriums," "Christopherian encounters," "multiple perspectivism," etc. I'm already turned off.

Gardner's description of the 5-10-year-old draws copiously on others' research. His stress on "the disjunctions between the intuitive and the scholastic minds," and the need for schools to confront them, has been anticipated by Susan Carey. Most of his remedies, as he admits, have been developed elsewhere.

Gardner has real *chutzpah*. He thinks that if this country is serious about educational reform, it would do well to implement his vision. Not even the progressive educators got that far. Gardner criticizes their "optimism" and claims that he can meet the needs they overlooked, notably to assess students and teachers and to motivate alienated children. Yet he does not address the conditions his program faces today: social decay, family breakup, tight money, entrenched bureaucracies, incompetent teachers, competing programs, and rationales for all sorts of proposals.

With the monocular vision characteristic of ed psychs, he expects this country to rebuild its educational system around an unproven theory of cognitive development. He cites favorable evidence from the Brunerite school but virtually none from other traditions. Doesn't he realize that psychology has spawned one doomed theory after another? Why should his own theory buck that trend? Worse, he proposes a psychological theory where a philosophic or multi-disciplinary theory is needed. In addition to Geertz, he should have consulted Habermas or Foucault. They would have shown him what a theory of social transformation might look like, especially since (as he emphasizes) you can't remold education unless you carry the community with you.

Gardner may appeal to ed psychs but he says little that experienced teachers don't know. His terms alone are new. Successful teachers already adapt formal knowledge to the student's informal understanding. A good English teacher invites her class to interpret fiction and not expect stereotypical heroes and villains. (That's Gardner's "multiple perspectivism.") The technological fixes he recommends ("thinker tool," "envisioning machine," "geometric supposer") are expensive toys for a need that already is met...by those who know how to teach. As I will show, William James's *Talks to Teachers* is a more useful guide than Gardner's pretentious tract. What we need today is a sequel to James's book by an Olympian scholar. Titled *Talks to Ed Psychs,* it would expose the froth that Gardner's book fails to dispel and inform ed psychs on what they must do to truly advance the theory and practice of education.

January 92

59

William James's "Talks to Teachers": Psychology with Philosophy in Education—1

aving reread William James's wise and eloquent *Talks to Teachers*, I cannot see what we have learned in ninety years of research that he has not already told us. For example, what teachers need most, says James, is an "adequate"conception of the child's nature:

I cannot but think that to apperceive your pupil as a little sensitive, impulsive, associative, and reactive organism, partly fated and partly free, will lead to a better intelligence of all his ways. Understand him, then, as such a subtle little piece of machinery. And if, in addition, you can also see him sub-specie boni and love him as well, you will be in the best position for becoming perfect teachers.

Thus James sums up the substance of his *Talks.* You may disagree with him. Yet no one, not Dewey, not Piaget, not a single ed psych, has portrayed the nature of the young learner more incisively and elegantly than this. And research has yet to prove him wrong. He writes:

What is the purpose of education? It is to produce thoughtful, capable people who know a great deal and can use what they know. The crucial question for any educational system to answer is, How broadly have its graduates learned and what difference has it made to them? So you see, the process of education, taken in a large way, may be described as nothing but the process of acquiring ideas or conceptions, the best educated mind being the mind which has the largest stock of them, ready to meet the largest possible variety of the emergencies of life. The lack of education means only the failure to have acquired them, and the consequent liability to be 'floored' and 'rattled' in the vicissitudes of experience.

Improve on that, my friends.

Although the curriculum should be "concrete and sensory," its prime aim is not to "lubricate things...and make them interesting" but to "stimulate" the child to think abstractly. Refuting "our modern reformers," James declares:

I myself, in dwelling so much upon the native impulses and object-teaching and anecdotes and all that, have paid my tribute to the line of least resistance.... Yet away back in childhood we find the beginnings of purely intellectual curiosity.... Object-teaching is mainly to launch the pupils, with some concrete conceptions of the facts concerned, upon the more abstract ideas.

Note that word "launch." What finer image for every primary curriculum?

What about "effort" and "interest"? Students, says James, will not make an effort unless they are interested. So how do you interest them? By communicating your interest in them, in the subject, and by following certain principles:

Elicit interest from within, by the warmth with which you care for the subject yourself and by following the laws I have laid down. If the topic be highly abstract, show its nature by concrete examples. If it be unfamiliar, trace some point of analogy in it with the known. If it be difficult, couple its acquisition with some prospect of personal gain.

Where can we find a better union of wisdom with advice? For more of both, read on.

January 1992

60

William James's "Talks to Techers": Psychology with Philosophy in Education—II

What do tests tell us? They measure the student's knowledge but not his drive to learn, which counts for more. "The total mental efficiency of a man," writes James, "is the resultant of the working together of all his faculties.... He is too complex a being for any of them to have the casting vote." What matters most is the intensity of his desires, the degree of interest he takes in a project. "Memory, concentration, reasoning power, inventiveness, excellence of the senses—all are subsidiary to this." Always bear in mind, he writes, that every child has an ego.

What part do instincts play? Like desires, instincts—such as rivalry, possessiveness, and pugnacity—should be roused and harnessed, not diverted into play. Take rivalry:

> *The wise teacher will use this instinct, as she uses others, reaping the advantages and appealing to it in such a way as to reap a maximum of benefit with a minimum of harm.... Respect, then, I beg you, always the original reactions, even when you are seeking to overcome their connection with certain objects, and to supplant these reactions with others that you wish to make the rule.*

119

True, teachers today face harsher emotions: aggression, alienation, racism, etc. James surely would have sympathized, but he would not have changed his mind. The passions, he held, have to be used, not denied. That is the challenge our teachers must meet.

What can psychology tell the teacher? What it can not tell the teacher is how to teach. "Psychology," says James, "is a science [sic] and teaching is an art; and sciences never generate arts directly out of themselves." Any psychological law is compatible with several teaching methods, hence it cannot dictate which of them to use. Psychology may establish laws of thought, but the teacher must decide how she will work with them. "Where the teacher's art begins," says James, "psychology cannot help in the least." The teacher's personality, her influence with her students, her on-the-spot inventiveness—these are among the attributes that count.

James was wrong on one crucial point. Psychology has not progressed as he expected. He believed that psychologists would uncover the laws of the mind. Instead psychology has lost itself in a vast delta of subfields and conflicting theories. There are no agreed-on psychological "laws" for teachers to follow, only the lore of the classroom that teachers learn from experience and from the example of other teachers.

Someone should write a "Pedagogy of the Informed" on the main disciplines that inform pedagogy: history, philosophy, anthropology, and literature. These are the studies that distinguish a reputable Graduate School of Education from an ordinary think tank.

February 1992

61

Men's Studies:
The Supreme Sacrifice
(Jeu D'Espirit Extraordinaire)

Two years ago, facing charges that Women's Studies were discriminatory, our Graduate School of Education launched a program of Men's Studies. Critics assailed the program on two grounds: that men's issues were amply covered by existing courses; and that enrollment in Women's Studies would plummet as women moved to be with men.

And move they did. Men's Studies attracted so many co-eds that Women's Studies folded for lack of interest.

The Men's program was designed to highlight the support—moral, emotional, and intellectual—that men have given women throughout history. Without the devotion of husbands and lovers, the human race would still be living in caves. While women led nations, campaigned for reforms, and created great works of art, science, and literature, men cooked, swept, changed diapers, and comforted their mates in times of grief. Sadly, some women drove their men to suicide.

As Men's Studies became controversial, faculty staged the infamous Shlock-Shlemihl Debate. Royce Hall was filled to capacity, mostly with women, yet ten minutes before the debate was to begin, the incredible happened. Half a dozen male chauvinists walked the aisles with tickets to Chippendales (the male strip club). The hall emptied in a flash, and the debate was cancelled. At the club police were called to keep order, and extra performances were laid on throughout the night. It was a triumph of libido.

Meantime, the husbands of the debaters rescued their deserted wives and played to the hilt their historic role of assuaging the female ego.

At length, out of sheer compassion, the faculty, too, played this role. They voted to eliminate Men's Studies and resurrect its predecessor. Thus was confirmed, once again, men's traditional role of supporting women. By becoming sensitized to the needs of women and empowering them, they deliberately sacrificed themselves. That's what being a *man* is all about!

The New Women's Studies: In a bow to the new sensitivity, the program now includes a unit on men's contributions to the success of women. And, per Affirmative Action, a MAN now heads the program! Men are signing up in droves, and everyone is in a state of bliss. Four cheers to MEN in Women's Studies!

February 1992

62

The Scheffler Factor—1

Israel Scheffler is one of the few writers on education who is read and admired by mainstream philosophers. Yet mainstream educationists find him recondite and remote. This is unfortunate because his ideas are powerful enough to redirect educational research and ultimately practice. Let me suggest why.

Scheffler's latest work, *In Praise of the Cognitive Emotions* (Routledge, 1991), brings together fourteen recent essays. In one of them he explains why we should educate two "specifically cognitive emotions": the surprise at the unexpected that tells the student he may be mistaken, and the joy of verification that tells him he may be right. Modern science harnesses these emotions, using the unexpected refutation to spur renewed thoughts, and the prospect of ultimate verification to stimulate more rigorous testing. Intellectual development—a process of learning and unlearning—depends on these emotions too, for the unwillingness to shed old beliefs is overcome by the expectation of joy in achieving better ones. "The growth of cognition," says Scheffler, "is thus inseparable from the education of the emotions."

Contrast Scheffler here with Howard Gardner (*Missive* 58). Gardner simply assumes that the emotions contribute to intellectual growth. Scheffler, on the other hand, develops an argument, backed by empirical evidence, for the intellectual importance of two specific research-driven emotions. He shows how science and intellectual growth use subjective processes to produce objective outcomes.

Scheffler is particularly persuasive on creative learning. In "Making and Understanding" he revises our notion of the creative process and updates the process method of learning, in which the student reenacts the creation of works he studies. The student, he argues, should treat the creative process not as a single act of creation but as a series of experimental tryouts and revisions which gradually bring the creator's purpose and its tentative outcome into harmony. Process learning now becomes truly educative, because it imitates the real process of creation rather than a stereotype. It also encourages the students to reflect on their own actions, many of which share the same experimental structure as the creative process itself.

In "Computers at School?" Scheffler shows how technological thinking shrinks our concepts. Terms appropriate to the mind, he contends, have been applied to computer simulations, and terms appropriate to simulations (such as "information") have then been applied to the mind. This "double transfer" impoverishes our understanding of mind and education alike. For example, the computer metaphor of mind excludes much that belongs to the ordinary notion of problem solving, such as perception, invention, wonder, conflict, and doubt. Hence, it cannot be used in formulating the problem-solving aim of education, still less such aims as the cultivation of insight, know-how, and character.

March 1992

63

The Scheffler Factor—II

Scheffler uses philosophic methods to untangle specific issues in education. In "Basic Mathematical Skills," for example, he examines a number of ambiguous concepts and outlines an empirical research program based on his analysis. He distinguishes between: (a) the subject matter of mathematics (an educators' construct) and the autonomous discipline; (b) mathematical methods (formal operations) and mathematical skills (mental processes involved in learning and applying these operations); (c) skills that are unique to mathematics and those it shares with other subjects; (d) deductive thinking (following a proof) and strategic thinking (reconstructing a proof); and (e) skills used to attain understanding and understanding itself (the achieved grasp of a topic). Few of these distinctions are made, let alone emphasized in courses on the teaching of mathematics.

Like William James (*Missives 59, 60*), Scheffler denies that there is any special relation between psychology and education. Claims made by psychologists do not apply automatically to education but must be weighed in the light of educational ideals. Like Wittgenstein (*Missive 72*), he warns that psychologists work with unanalyzed assumptions and loaded terms. For example, unless the meanings of "learning" are identified and defined, the claims of different learning theories cannot be examined or compared. Scheffler also demolishes the computer model of mind, on which Gardner relies uncritically. At the same time he welcomes any psychology that is intellectually coherent, empirically confirmed, and relevant to education—of which, let me add, there is very little. *(Missives 38, 39, 58)*

Scheffler writes more for academicians than ordinary teachers, and readers must work as hard to understand his ideas as he did to produce them. His painstaking analyses are conveyed in intricate, knotted prose. Reading him reminds me of Milton's jibe, "How harsh is crabbed philosophy." Although he examines concrete problems, he displays no interest in the way those they involve feel about them. His most ambitious essay, "Human Nature and Potential," barely registers the emotional significance, the hope and frustration invested, in the reality it treats. This work, in fact, needs an interpreter, one who will state its message for education in terms to which educationists can respond...as I have tried to do here.

Nevertheless, this wide-ranging work is a challenge to pedagogues and ed psychs alike. Unlike most of them, Scheffler relies on sound arguments and common sense backed by empirical research. Essay by essay he thinks through key educational issues, showing that they are complex yet solvable. He dismantles problems that Gardner either overlooks or handles superficially. Work like Scheffler's is the best stimulus to educational inquiry. It is a foundation that educationists can build on. This volume alone is worth a stack of ed psych tracts and a truckload of the usual pedagogical pedantry.

March 1992

64

Choosing Choice

ritics of school choice have become hysterical. Choice, they cry, is a "monster with its foot in the door," an epidemic that will kill public education. No way. Public schooling is rooted too deeply in our culture to be dislodged. Choice is a shot in the arm for it, not a *coup de grâce.*

If you don't want choice, you can choose not to have it; but if you don't like public education, you end up paying for it anyhow. Over two-thirds of Americans are said to favor choice, including a good majority of the so-called "underprivileged."

Critics complain that choice applies free-market principles where they don't belong. Not so. Choice applies some market principles to a certain extent, and they work well. The education market is not unlike a market of many competing firms. Choice stimulates this market by encouraging schools to compete and diversify in order to attract customers.

They also claim that education is not a true market since schools, unlike firms, rarely shut down. Students, after all, have to be educated somewhere. Under choice, however, some schools will shut down, as other, more competitive schools attract more students. Entrepreneurs then enter either to take over schools ready for Chapter 11 or to found new ones where there is a demand.

Critics fear that choice will stratify our public schools the way it does their private counterparts, with the "best" schools drawing the most talented students and the rest ranging from average to nowhere. This need not happen. Standards for racial, ethnic, and economic balance already are written into law, and they always can be strengthened. Also, many parents value ideals other than intellectual excellence—such as personal growth, artistic expression, vocational preparation, and social responsibility, which some schools satisfy more than others.

Choice backers are accused of being "elitist." That's supposed to clinch the argument. Elite schools, it's said, will nourish the upper strata of American education by sucking talent and resources from further down. Yet the opposite scenario is more likely. Elite schools are natural pacesetters. They stimulate others to try harder and thus help raise the standards of all. Isn't America, after all, a society of pacesetters? Isn't competition, fundamentally, the American way?

Will choice privatize American education? Will it obliterate any real difference between public and private schools? Not at all. Public schools are a bastion of the welfare state; they are melting pots of an increasingly diversified population; and bureaucrats will fight to defend them. Remember, too, that many public schools are better than many private ones. They will prosper whether there is choice or not. And no government is going to abandon them.

April 1992

65

How to Solve
Educational Problems

As most of us know, dealing with educational problems can be a problem in itself. Here are some hints on how to succeed.

◆ Always profess not to have the answer. That proves you are intellectually modest and lets you out of having any answer at all.

◆ If you can't answer a question, say it is covered in another course, and discussing it here would lead to misunderstanding.

◆ Warn your students of the dangers involved in drawing quick conclusions—dangers like exceeding your authority, asserting more than is definitely known, misusing data, or incurring rejection. Smile smugly and say, "We really don't have the answers. Further research is needed."

◆ Retreat into various ways of approaching the problem. If it deals with theory, turn to philosophy, even though you never took a course in it. In this way you can talk the problem to death.

◆ Talk about general objectives on which all can agree. This will suggest that no changes need be made. The main problem then will be to justify the *status quo*, which always has been difficult.

♦ Use such bromides as "in a Pickwickian sense," or "other things being equal," or "in one sense or another," all of which say nothing and can be interpreted any old way. If you or your students say "ya know," it means you or they may not.

♦ Use circular arguments, which drop you happily back to where the discussion started. For example, announce that you're going to define the nature of a core course. Conclude that it's all in the content.

♦ Tell students that in this, the world's greatest democracy, they must learn to solve their own problems. You may even suggest that in other countries students are not encouraged to think for themselves. (That's why the Japanese are so uncreative!)

♦ If students doubt you, tell them you have used your "solution" for at least ten years, even though you haven't. This will reassure them that the problem has been solved and that there's nothing more to worry about.

♦ Always conclude by saying: "Even if the problem hasn't been solved, all of you have clarified your thinking, and that's what it's all about."

Summer 1992

66

Multiculturalism: The Rainbow and the Pot of Gold

ulticulturalists maintain that knowledge varies with culture; what is true in one culture is not always true in another. But what does "multi" mean? How many more than one? Hollywood High School has students of some sixty different cultures. How many multicultural teachers will we need to care for these sixty cultures?

For starters, what is "culture"? It is an integrated pattern consisting of at least fourteen elements: social structures, languages, laws, ethics, politics, religions, schools, art, science, technology, beliefs, aspirations, magic, enlightenment, etc., in no special order. So now we have sixty cultures, each with fourteen elements, for a total of 840 units!

We're not finished. To create a subject matter, a teachable content, out of multiculturalism, we would have to structure and integrate the units within each pattern, and then relate both units and patterns to the subject matter representing the dominant culture. These are formidable, if not impossible, tasks. What mortal is prepared to tackle them? Or do we need a supercomputer?

What are the sources of multicultural knowledge? They are: many languages, world history, universal philosophy, comparative literature, cultural anthropology, comparative and international education. All this knowledge would have to be integrated, organized in such a way as to make it teachable and amenable to scholarly investigation.

There also would be many crucial issues that would have to be addressed, among them: race, religion, gender, poverty, literacy, which, though treatable in established disciplines, would require serious and special attention in multicultural courses.

Where do we find the teachers? The researchers? Ninety-five percent of teachers and teachers of teachers are monolingual and monocultural. Teachers may be multiculturally motivated and well-meaning, but how knowledgeable can they be if they are monolingual and monocultural? And how long will it take for future teachers to acquire the necessary disciplines and languages? Most educationists today are little interested in languages other than English.

A university's central concern is the pursuit and dissemination of substantive knowledge. Embracing the cause of multiculturalism is not enough. No matter how urgent or desirable the cause, advocacy and propagandization have no place. Lay organizations abound where multiculturalism can be promoted, and in whatever fashion they choose. Some day teachers may appear who are truly multicultural and who, even modestly, can meet the requirements as set forth here. That may be "somewhere over the rainbow," and no "pot of gold" has yet been seen in this our worldly existence.

Summer 1992

67

Student Values in American Universities

ome time ago I addressed a group of professors from UCLA's professional schools on student values in our universities. Here is a summary, updated, of my remarks.

Students live socially and emotionally as well as intellectually. They face the inner conflicts of their age group in surroundings that are both stressful and stimulating. Often they are ambivalent about what they learn, needing to value it yet reluctant to do so.

Students do not assume that a course is "good" for them just because it is offered. They value intellectual achievement as an end in itself, as an aspect of personal growth, and as an entree to a career. Few, however, will sacrifice everything to it. They have other priorities they deem more important.

So what do university students value today? How do they compare with previous generations? Some values have endured, others are waning, others still have come to the fore.

◆ **Enduring Values.** The values still admired include independence (moral and intellectual), social responsibility (especially toward the disadvantaged), social justice (equal treatment regardless of race, religion, sex, and income), and determination to succeed.

◆ **Receding Values**. Some values on the way out are family cohesion, patriotism, extreme rationalism, pure science, and organized religion.

◆ **Emerging Values**. Incoming values are self-expression, the "fun ethic," the quest for experience (through travel, public service, sex, drugs, etc.), international cooperation, appreciation of human differences, and professional success.

Some of these three types of value have persisted over time but with varying degrees of emphasis. Also different students weigh values differently, depending on whether the students are "activist," "uncommitted," "alienated," "apathetic," "square," "queer," or "reactionary."

Should teachers declare their own values? Yes, within reason. These values are going to emerge anyway, so why not make them explicit? Teachers and students then know where they stand, and genuine intellectual encounter is possible.

Summer 1992

68

Isms, Studies, Hyphenates

Professors should be more clear about what can and cannot be taught in a university. Take feminism, bilingualism, multiculturalism, women's studies, African-Americanism, Asian-Americanism, and the like. What would I do if I were to teach them? In what way do they belong in a university curriculum?

That depends on what you mean by "teaching," a topic that has provoked more than its share of debate. I will simply say that teaching does not mean telling, much less pontificating. It means imparting knowledge in the tradition of great universities, so that those who receive it will become better persons (*Missive 22*).

Given this meaning, I would have a problem teaching feminism, bilingualism, and multiculturalism, because I would find little substantive knowledge I could impart. As these various "isms" relate to the subject matter of education, all available knowledge could be covered in a single lecture. The rest would be opinion—the stuff of rallies and talk shows, of little value in a university.

Women's studies, on the other hand, would be too much for me to handle, because they involve all fields of knowledge. As a philosopher, I could teach the ideas of some women educators, but I would have to let our historians handle women's studies in the way they deal with nearly everything.

How about hyphenates? It's hard to specify what African-American studies should include. In Africa there are over a hundred different languages, dialects, cultures, and political entities. They are less united than the nations of Europe, which are divided enough. I could teach the ideas of some black educators, but I doubt that I could find many African precedents to which appeal so often is made.

The problem is even more acute for Asian-American studies. What Koreans would say that they were enough like Japanese to let anyone teach their respective cultures as if they were similar? In consideration of the wide variations among the many cultures of Asia, the teaching problem becomes increasingly complicated. I could teach Japanese educational theories or those of other countries. I perhaps could engage in a comparative study. But even if I were a dedicated Asian-American, I couldn't begin to handle all studies going by that name.

Faced with these problems, I conclude that the best course is to absorb all these "isms" and hyphenates into the established disciplines. Even if it were feasible to teach them separately, the effect would be to divide, rather than unify, the curriculum and the university community. Instead of tacking material onto the intellectual frameworks we have, let's include it within that framework and thus enrich it.

Summer 1992

69

True Breadth

ince degrees are awarded by the University, rather than departments, the Graduate Council of the University has stipulated that breadth courses be required for the award of the PhD. There are five types of breadth in the Graduate School of Education that clearly do not stretch the mind and one that does.

◆ **Administrative–Style Breadth.** Since the GSE is structured by specialties, each specialization, it is said, should have its own breadth course. This is *false* because specialties are not alike. Special education, for instance, is a far cry from history, and guidance and counseling, to its cost, has little in common with philosophy.

◆ **Politicized Breadth.** Because we believe in academic freedom, democratic participation, and equal opportunity, professors allegedly should be free to teach breadth courses as they see fit. *False*, because breadth is an academic, not a political concept, and democracy has nothing to do with it.

◆ **Practical Breadth.** Because in some specialties enrollments are low, they can be boosted by adding breadth courses. *False*. The aim of breadth courses is to broaden

137

the mind, not to make up for deficiencies in staffing or enrollments.

◆ **Personalized Breadth.** Because the GSE serves students, breadth courses should be tailored to the needs of individual students. *False.* The purpose of breadth is to gain knowledge that individuals may not realize they need but should have as GSE graduates.

◆ **Breadth as Enrichment.** Breadth courses allegedly should be closely related to a student's specialty. For instance, a student majoring in curriculum should take breadth courses in child psychology, say, or guidance and counseling, or learning and instruction. *False.* These fields are subdivisions of the general field of educational psychology, and the courses they offer are basic to themselves. At best, they would be "enrichment" courses.

◆ **Breadth as Knowledge.** The true purpose of breadth courses is to provide PhD students with knowledge basic to the entire field of education. This knowledge is mainly theoretical, normative, issue-oriented, and aimed at decision-making and policy formation. In the GSE the only true breadth courses belong to history, philosophy, literature, and the human sciences. All the rest are professional, vocational, skill-developing, etc. However, majors in disciplinary fields might do well to take a breadth course in curriculum, say, or higher education, or administration, assuming the emphasis in these courses is on policy formation.

Summer 1992

70

Foucault on Education

Truth. Like other postmodernists, French philosopher Michel Foucault holds that "truth" is an expression of sectional interests. Different groups have different ideas of the truth, but those groups with most power (the "elites" or the "ruling class") make their "truth" prevail through their control of key institutions like schools and colleges, the media, and the law. Truth ultimately is what those in power want you to believe. Thus truth is intimately connected with the exercise of power. As Foucault puts it:

> It's not a matter of emancipating truth from every system of power (which would be a chimera, for truth already is power) but of detaching the power of truth from the forms of hegemony, social, economic, and cultural, within which it operates at the present time.

Knowledge. Schools impart knowledge that helps us understand the world, classify our experiences, and perceive things, *all in the approved way.* They give us the official version of reality and they make it stick, mostly by suppressing other ways of understanding the world. Thus all thought is political. It expresses the interest of one side or another in a perpetual struggle. And all knowledge is contingent, uncertain, transitory..."destined even for oblivion." In a world increasingly gripped by violence, injustice, and decay we must recognize that knowledge is both uncertain and controlled.

Reason. Foucault says we are starry-eyed. We fool ourselves that some day freedom and compassion will replace social and cultural oppression. We do not realize that a change of this magnitude requires an independence of mind that the institutions of our culture make almost impossible. We are fooled especially by the media that turn the world into a daylong Disneyland, a souped-up, sanitized "reality" of their own. They offer no higher vision of life, no rational representation of just and authentic human relations. We dwell in a world of *un*reason.

Education. The school is like an asylum, says Foucault, a means through which the state creates a compliant, hardworking population. He cites three "instruments" through which the school exercises "disciplinary power." They are "hierarchical observation," "normalizing judgment," and, above all, the "examination." *Hierarchical observation* is the process of keeping students under constant surveillance. *Normalizing judgment* is the assessment of student performance against norms taken from the human sciences. The *examination* combines these two instruments, since here the empowered (teachers) observe the powerless (students) and seek to extract performances that match the norms desired. What, then, *should* we teach? That, unknown to us, our words and thoughts express powerful interests of race, gender, religion, and class.

Critique. What are we to make of all this? Intermittently original, Foucault also is willfully perverse. The murk of his prose yields hardly a glimmer of common sense. His notion of power is almost impenetrable. Obsessed with bureaucratic France, he vastly exaggerates the state's grip on the teacher and the teacher's on her class. For most American students exams are not a *rite de passage* but a pain in the butt. Nor is reality sliced any way the power structure pleases. His American acolytes, Giroux and McLaren, are equally "off the wall." U.S. teachers are not the robots of Foucault's fantasies.

Fall 1992

71

Heidegger:
Being, Thinking, Educating

ne of the greatest philosophers of our time was also one of its outstanding teachers. Martin Heidegger (1889-1975) was original and unforgettable. As his student, Hannah Arendt wrote, "In Heidegger...thinking has come to life again. The cultural treasures of the past, believed to be dead, are being made to speak."

In 1933 the riveting, bike-riding professor in peasant dress was unanimously elected Rector of the University of Freiburg. In his inaugural address, which I heard, he urged the university to renew itself spiritually and lead the renewal of the German people. He resigned a year later, frustrated by the pressures of the regime. He was not a political animal.

Heidegger was obsessed with the nature of "Being." He portrayed it not as a thing or a process but as a "light" or "clearing" in which things "present themselves" as they really are. We humans, he said, should regard ourselves not as independent knowers of external things but as their partners in a realm of Being that embraces all alike. Knowledge acquired by treating things as targets of inquiry yields power over them and corrupts the knower. Exploited intellectually and then technologically, things become a "standing reserve" from which humans extract maximum advantage with minimum effort. Nature is despoiled; society disintegrates, and man no longer is the "shepherd of Being."

How can education reorient us to Being? One way is to preserve traditional practices like craftsmanship, nature study, and festivals. Schools must resist reforms that encourage the exploitation of people and things, like managerial training and business techniques. We must create a new focus of benign practices that will strengthen our ties to the earth (as the temples did in classical Greece).

Another response is to encourage *meditative thinking* which allows things to appear to us in their true nature. When we meditate, we do not simply look at things but recall them, for it is only in retrospect that experiences disclose their full meaning. For Proust, the quest for the meaning of lost time underlies *A la recherche du temps perdu*, one of the greatest of all French novels.

Schools must foster meditative thinking as an end in itself. The meditative thinker dwells as naturally in the mind's realm as the woodcutter in the wood that he fashions. Many students may be too impatient to meditate but in Heidegger's view, all are capable. We all intrinsically are "thinking, that is, meditating beings."

Literature, too, recalls us to Being. At its best, poetry is "richer" than philosophy and packed with more meaning. Poets tap the primal senses of words, which evoke what they name more powerfully than later, acquired meanings. Through language, poems let the things they name exhibit themselves to the mind in their true form.

Heidegger's legacy stimulated pathbreaking work in fields from physics (Heisenberg) to literary criticism (De Man). He inspired new schools of psychoanalysis (May, Binswanger) and new movements in theology (Bultmann, Rahner). He was a major influence on Paul Celan, one of the greatest postwar poets in the German language. He also invigorated such areas as nursing, ecology, software (Winograd), and artificial intelligence critique (Dreyfus). Sadly, he lacks appeal to educationists obsessed with ethnicity, multiculturalism, inclusion, and empowerment. But his thought will outline all such concerns.

Fall 1992

72

Wittgenstein:
Words and Their Meanings

A solitary, self-tormenting genius is unlikely to make a good teacher. Yet Ludwig Wittgenstein (1889–1951) tried hard. On leaving the army he trained as an elementary school teacher and then spent six years in village schools in lower Austria. With bright students he was enthusiastic, tutoring them after hours and taking them on outings. With others he was impatient. Wrote one student, "Witkinstein (*sic*) is an impossible man. Every time you say something, he says,'No, no, that's not the point.'" The parents, mostly farmers, disliked his arrogance and harsh discipline, and he in turn loathed their provincialism. Under pressure from parents he resigned. This period as a teacher influenced his later philosophy more than has been acknowledged.

Professor: In Cambridge, England, during the 1930s Wittgenstein taught small groups of students in his room. Instead of lecturing, he spoke extempore in monologues broken by long silences, in which he racked his brain for insights. Afterward he would dash to a movie, usually a western, for relief. A colleague called him "a man who is quite incapable of carrying on a discussion." His students were awed by him, becoming clones of the master rather than independent thinkers (but what clones!).

Philosopher: Throughout his career, Wittgenstein sought to account for the meaning of words. Language, he said, is like a box of tools with many purposes, only one of which is making statements. Philosophic puzzles are not about matters

143

of ultimate fact but arise from linguistic misunderstandings, from our failure to examine closely the words in which our problems are posed. Hence philosophy should become "a battle against the bewitchment of intelligence by means of language." It is a form of therapy which uses certain techniques to dispel verbal confusion and "show the fly (of intelligence) the way out of the bottle (of language)."

Educationist: Take the question, What is education? Because the question looks like What is sunlight?, it tempts us to seek some process or thing we can point to and describe, as we can sunlight. Hence the endless theories of education since Plato. The question we ought to ask is, How is the word "education" used in different contexts? For Wittgenstein the meaning of "education" and of most other words is the sum total of their uses in the language. To pinpoint the meanings of a word, Wittgenstein suggests asking: How is this word learned? How would we put it across to a child? Children, he says, are trained in language games rather than taught. They are told how to use certain words rather than given reasons for using them. They are not told why they are to use these words rather than others. However, teaching with reasons does not begin until the children know enough to ask questions about what they are being taught. Until then they must trust the teacher. The young child, says Wittgenstein, believes the teacher. Doubt comes only after belief.

Legacy: The problems of philosophy have not dissolved under analysis, as Wittgenstein forecast they would, and many philosophers still propose the theories and use the techniques he repudiated. Nevertheless, Wittgenstein above all is responsible in large part for philosophy's current preoccupation with language. His influence in the philosophy of education has been immense, for education is a relatively nontechnical affair and hence one especially suited to ordinary–language analysis. (Teachers do talk a lot—perhaps too much, as John Goodlad tells us.) As University of California, Berkeley, philosopher John Searle declares, "Wittgenstein, in spite of himself, is largely responsible for the opportunities that have opened up (in recent philosophy)."

Fall 1992

73

Where's the Logos in Ed Psych?

At UCLA, as elsewhere, most educational psychologists think small and teach what the job market requires. Their research is little different from that done in the state colleges. Why, with money so tight, we employ so many of them is one of the mysteries of our time.

Most educational psychologists admit that their discipline rests on philosophy, yet they refuse to act accordingly. Most don't know enough philosophy to do so, don't understand what the relationship entails, don't want to make the effort, don't wish to make their work less "practical," and balk at changing the habits of a lifetime. Yet the fact remains that all major psychologists have used philosophy to inspire and justify their work.

Although psychology declared its independence late in the 19th century, only the style of research changed, not the substance. William James pronounced the verdict: "There is no 'new (scientific) psychology' worthy of the name.... There is nothing but the old psychology, which began in Locke's time (philosophy of mind), plus a little physiology of the brain and senses and a few introspective details."

Freud, it is true, blamed philosophers for overvaluing logic and ignoring the unconscious. Yet he was a strict positivist himself and, later, a speculative philosopher meditating, like Nietzsche and Schopenhauer, on the human condition. "My

145

discoveries are the basis for a very grave philosophy," he said. "There are very few who understand this."

Piaget called his research institute The International Center for Genetic Epistemology. "I'm not a psychologist," he said, "I'm an epistemologist." Genetic epistemology "has as its object the formation of knowledge, that is, of the cognitive relations between subject and object." Piaget was, in fact, a neo-Kantian, much indebted to French philosophers, such as Claparède, who replaced Kant's twelve categories of the mind with concepts more useful to science. Piaget also was a structuralist who traced the formal, logical relations between space, time, number, quantity, and other concepts. Instead of modeling the child's actual behavior, he charted the knowledge and the conceptual structures underlying that behavior at different stages of development. These structures are epistemological, not psychological. They are formed by the logical relations between concepts—relations that are uncovered by abstract reflection, not empirical research. Ed psychs teach only the genetic strand in Piaget and believe it's the whole.

Jerome Bruner said recently that psychology of mind cannot be free of philosophy of mind. "If philosophy is concerned with the alternative ways in which we can formulate our concepts and our language, about the nature and uses of mind, we must obviously be in partnership with philosophy...." Bruner calls Freud, Piaget, and Vygotsky "the three modern titans of development theory." These titans, role models for ed psychs, all were philosophers at heart. In this Graduate School of Education you would never know it.

Fall 1992

146

74

Vygotsky: Enlightened Marxist

ike William James, Piaget, and Freud, Bolshevik Lev Semenovich Vygotsky (1896-1934) was a global, multidisciplinary thinker. Though he worked in psychology, he was at heart a philosopher (as he himself said) with a deep interest in literature, language, and anthropology. His basic ideas came from outside psychology and especially from Marxist philosophy. His method of genetic explanation, taken from Marx, seeks to identify the basic units in terms of which more complex psychological phenomena can be understood. For Vygotsky, these units—the "microcosms of human consciousness"—are word meanings, since language is the decisive influence on human development. Education, in which children learn to use language in recognized ways, is the prime medium for transmitting culture and hence promoting development.

For Vygotsky, following Marx, mental functioning originates in social functioning, in the speech and actions of others. "The first great problem [of psychology]," he wrote, "is to show how the individual response emerges from the forms of collective life." The child matures by internalizing culture acquired through social interaction. Education, then, is not only acculturation but enculturation. The individual is a cultural product.

This thesis, the sociocultural formation of the child, gives Vygotsky his key educational idea: the "zone of proximal development." He defines this zone as the distance between "the actual developmental level (of the child) as determined by independent problem solving" and the level of "potential development as determined through problem–solving under adult guidance or in collaboration with more capable peers." Education is the process of helping the student to pass continuously from actual to potential levels of development. Education promotes psychological growth through the assimilation of culture. It follows, for Vygotsky, that "the only 'good learning' is that which is *in advance* of development, that which makes the individual what he is not but can be."

For Vygotsky the study of literature is crucial. Literature, he held, can form and change the mind by "defamiliarizing" reality, so that one looks at the world "through new eyes." Revisioning the world, he says, enables us to learn what we did not notice before.

Teachers also should study anthropology. As a young man Vygotsky had visited Uzbekistan and Kirghizstan to study the thinking of collective farmers. He concluded that culture makes a decisive difference to intelligence. Thus he takes a much broader view of the self than most Western psychologists. Instead of explaining the self and its acts in terms of intrapsychic factors such as drives, motives, and learning capacities, he places the self in a social space where it transacts and negotiates with others.

Russian (later Harvard) linguist and critic Roman Jacobson called Vygotsky "more literary and philosophical than psychological." And, I would add, more anthropological than our ed psychs appreciate. Vygotsky is not the democratic Western psychologist they present to their students but an enlightened, humanist Marxist. As a developmentalist, he is in another sphere from Piaget and Kohlberg.

Most of the work done on Vygotsky by ed psychs today is irrelevant, unauthentic, and untrue to the thought of a great philosophic anthropologist.

Fall 1992

75

Philosophy in Cognitive Science

Cognitive science is a synthesis of philosophy, psychology, linguistics, artificial intelligence, and neurophysiology. Philosophy is the driving force of the synthesis, imparting analysis and imagination, rigor and excitement. It is distinguished from the other contributors mainly by the depth and abstractness of its questions. How does philosophy drive this discipline? Partly by analyzing assumptions, theories, and concepts in the field, but also by proposing empirically testable theories of its own. For example, in *The Modularity of the Mind* (1983), Jerry Fodor assumes that the mind is a computer program run on the hardware of the brain. The mind, he argues, comprises many different agencies—such as central processor systems, input systems, and sense organs—all working together. He maintains that the input systems that analyze sensory data are detached from the senses. Reflecting on philosophic theses about the mind, advancing and refuting philosophic arguments, and taking into account the known scientific facts, Fodor proposes a scientifically testable theory about the structure and functioning of the mind.

In *Consciousness Explained* (1991), philosopher Daniel Dennett insists that the discoveries of the neural sciences are insufficient to yield a theory of the mind. As he reviews these discoveries, he weaves a series of histories, analogies, thought experiments, and other devices into what he presents as "a single, coherent vision...a theory of the biological mechanisms (of the brain) and a way of thinking that will let you see how the traditional paradoxes and mysteries of consciousness can be resolved." Dennett's theory seeks to "explain every possible feature of consciousness within the framework of contemporary physical science." It is philosophic theory compatible with current neuroscience. What scientists do, he says, is to try to "figure out how the results of everybody's experiments blend imperceptively with what philosophers do."

Some cognitive scientists coming from the empirical sciences also have looked to philosophy. In *Understanding Computers and Cognition* (1986), Terry Winograd and Fernando Flores find in Martin Heidegger "a new understanding of how to design computer tools suited to human use and human progress." Heidegger, they say, is "the modern philosopher who has done the most thorough, penetrating, and radical analysis of everyday experience." (Winograd now teaches Heidegger in his Stanford computer classes.) Theories from science and engineering, they hold, tell us less about technology than philosophic theories of human existence, language, and action, which exert "a profound influence on what we build and how we use it."

"In psychology," said Wittgenstein, "there are experimental methods but conceptual confusion." Right on! Psychologists let their methods dictate what they discover. Instead of trying to find out how the mind actually works, they look for ways in which it resembles their models. Oversimplification and an obsession with design are the vices of our ed psychs. They should own up to the philosophic assumptions which shape their work. Instead of operating within a limited scientistic model of the mind, they should use a clearly–argued philosophic theory. Without one, their work will remain sterile and irrelevant, the dross of schools of education everywhere.

Fall 1992

76

The GSE's Assault on Disciplinary Knowledge

A while ago I conferred with some colleagues on the content of lower division seminars in education. They saw no need for a course in "Foundations," preferring "Current Problems" leading to "Practical Policies." No need for courses in history or philosophy either. Teachers could "bring them in" when needed, if at all. Moreover, they said, since those subjects already are taught in other departments, why should the Graduate School of Education teach them too?

This view ignores the logic of subject matter and threatens the reputation of our discipline. By the same token we could argue that there is no need for special studies since historians and philosophers could "bring them in" where appropriate, if at all.

How can students master history and philosophy if they pick them up on the way—a bit here and a bit there? Is this how specialists want their subjects taught? Can we learn math solely by studying science?

It is scandalous that except for psychology, disciplinary knowledge is so blithely downplayed in the schools of education. As they get down to their "practicalities," faculty routinely hand out a mix of half truth, distorted truth, odds and ends, and utterly mistaken advice. Students consume the stuff unaware that it contains no intellectual nourishment whatever.

Clearly, teachers should not teach what they do not know. If rank-and-file educationists, for whatever reasons, do not know much history and philosophy, their first obligation is to attain an adequate command of these subjects before they undertake to teach them. Once having crossed that threshold of mastery, they should go beyond the history and philosophy they think their students need to know and teach the fundamental aspects of these disciplines in and of themselves.

The Dean would like us to spread the word on the value of educational studies to our colleagues elsewhere on campus. An excellent idea that I long have advocated. But unless we spread the disciplines taught in the GSE, few will listen. Before we seek out our colleagues, we should learn a thing or two about the logical order of subject matter and the logical order of teaching it.

The GSE is supposed to teach teachers what and how to teach. Yet it's plain that we do this no better than teachers in other departments. In fact, some instructors on this campus can teach *us* how to teach. Very little of our research to date has any significance for other scholars or for the proper conduct of the University as a whole. Anyone who thinks otherwise is welcome to prove me wrong.

Fall 1992

77

The Golden Fleece Award for Useless Research

ver the years I have collected examples of useless research and nominated their authors for the award of the Golden Fleece. My folders bulge with the stuff. I have just pulled out a dilly that begs for a one-page *Missive*. Most defy rational summary.

A couple of educational psychologists, researching "social intelligence in children," want to study their ability to "recognize human emotions conveyed in facial expressions." They need photographs of young faces expressing joy, anger, puzzlement, etc. They will "pilot-test" these photos to "develop a measure of social intelligence." They want a dozen kids to face the camera.

Yet merely snapping the kids may affect them more than anything the researchers say. Even adults act differently before a camera. They powder their noses, straighten their ties, smile or swagger, depending on the purpose of the photograph. Will the kids be told what their photos are for? If so, won't their expressions be posed for the purpose? And if they are not told, how do we justify taking the photos?

Suppose parents are on hand. How will that affect their children? Won't the kids make faces to please or annoy mom and dad?

What is the point of "pilot-testing"? Unless we have a measure to assess the one we want to develop, what will we get out of the test? And if we already have a measure, why bother to develop this one? What is this "measure" anyway? It's not defined in the proposal.

What will this project tell us about education? Nothing is said on this point. Again, the proposal assumes we know what "social intelligence" is. Yet there are many societies and many intelligences. If it is the "ability to get along with others," what others and how? By this definition a gangbanger is blessed with social intelligence, since he gets on well with his gang (or else!). Do all parents want their kids to get along with everyone? How desirable is this intelligence? Some of our smartest kids don't socialize.

Why do we tolerate this mockery of scholarship? It's a waste of public funds and an insult to our discipline.

Fall 1992

78

The GSE Eight-Year Review (1992): Data Processing at Its Worst

aculty have been asked to respond to this *Review* before it descends on UCLA's Graduate Council. Few will, because an adequate response would require a lot of frustrating work. So what can be said in a single page?

Well, the *Review* has been carefully proofread. Grammar, punctuation, and spelling are correct; topic heads and paragraph leads neatly divide the terrain. Technically it is a finished job in an age that finishes little. As for the rest:

◆ The text is bloated with detail and swollen with statistics. It is systems analysis run amok.

◆ It is studded with repetitious, self-evident statements. All could have been said in less than half the space. The weight is in the paper, not in the thought.

◆ Truisms and circularity are everywhere, *e.g.*: "Enrollments are smaller due to fewer admissions." "When the number of courses increases we have more choice." "Funding depends on budgetary limits."

◆ Many statements (*e.g.*, on uneven course enrollments) are defended minimally or not at all.

◆ Terms are misdefined, *e.g.*, psychology is not a life science but a human science (if that).

◆ Pages 101, 104, 105, and 108 form a chorus of the self-evident.

◆ The page on "Weaknesses" is one of the weakest. Three weaknesses are conditions over which the Graduate School of Education has virtually no control. Absent are those weaknesses that the GSE can correct. They are obstacles to the GSE's mission in a University that is otherwise the envy of the world.

◆ The page on "Future Challenges" is a rehash. The authors obviously had burned out. They should study *Missive 47* on how to achieve distinction.

So what if the language sprawls, you say, so long as we get the drift? "Drift" is the word for it, ideas adrift in a swell of words. What we have is not a scholar's creation; it might have been slung together by a committee of bureaucrats. It is tumid with numbers and cliches, raw material that a legislator's aide can rake through to give his boss "the picture."

Some picture! It's a capitulation to the lowest nuts–and–bolts mentality of systems engineering. It virtually ignores the GSE's special mission in a world of disintegrating schools and colleges. It supplies the kind of quantitative data that any GSE could turn out in any institution of higher learning. It's the product of a think tank.

This *Review* reveals that UCLA's GSE has no distinctive character whatever. It's no more than a run-of-the-mill educational organization.

December 1992

79

John Goodlad
on "Education 2000"

nyone who thought that former colleague John Goodlad was headed for the Pacific twilight zone can think again. His latest essay, "On Taking School Reform Seriously" (*Phi Delta Kappan*, November 1992), is the finest on its subject yet. If all of us wrote as well, our Graduate School of Education would top the charts.

Goodlad argues that Education 2000, the drive to give this country a world-class educational system by century's end, must ally itself with grassroots reform. Aiming to restructure the educational system through national goals and tests, Education 2000, he says, barely considers the nuts and bolts of reeducating the young. The grassrooters, on the other hand, are full of ideas about the classroom but neglect the system as a whole. Each group needs the other.

Goodlad exposes two assumptions of Education 2000: first, that tests will be accurate enough for a high school diploma to deliver all the qualities that employers need in an employee; second, that the need to maintain world-class standards will ensure enough test-failers to do the unskilled labor for the rest of us. But, as Goodlad points out, if tests alone open the door to higher jobs and further education, parents soon will blame teachers, schools, and administrators for failing to deliver the knowledge required to pass them. Their lawyers will hit the ground running and the courts will go into gridlock. Are we ready to face this?

Goodlad refutes the charge that slumping scores on college entrance tests kicked the U.S. economy into reverse. "Healthy nations have healthy schools," he writes, "but schools are only one of many elements that keep a nation healthy." He reminds us how much education occurs outside schools—at home, among peers, on the playing field, on TV, in the work place, and (I might add) in church.

He warns that using schools for social engineering places them in "double jeopardy." Schools take the rap for problems (*e.g.*, crime, unemployment) over which they have little control. Then, when academic standards fall as resources shift to social engineering, schools are blamed for that too. He recommends the following steps to break the repeated cycle from euphoria to disillusion over education:

◆ Choose educative goals over social ones.

◆ Welcome grassroots reform.

◆ Treat parents, teachers, and principals as equal partners in reform.

◆ Admit that teachers need to run schools before they can reform them.

◆ Abandon the idea that school reform alone will solve the nation's ills.

Goodlad endorses Education 2000 but calls for an alliance with grassroots reformers. "Top-down needs bottom-up," he says. Without it, Education 2000 may restructure schools but will not re-educate students. Clearly, John Goodlad is on the right track in smart Seattle, home to Boeing, Nirvana, and two thriving educational institutes, both of which he heads. Sorry you left us, John. Stop by some day!

December 1992

80

A Grant-Free Evaluation #2

esponses to my *Missives* continue to pour in. Here are excerpts from some recent arrivals:

◆ "Thanks much for #79. Reach for 100!"

◆ "You are not liked by some of your colleagues because you force them to question their assumptions and thus demolish their research."

◆ "Why do you keep composing these *Missives*? I'm sure not all your colleagues read them.... They are too disturbing.... You are not going to change the faculty.... Many wish you would go away."

◆ "Keep up the *Missives*. They are instructive. It seems you will teach till your dying day."

◆ "I like the *Missives* that deal with today's educational problems. Some others are quite abstract, though I suppose they will endure longer for that reason."

◆ "Your *Missives* are valuable because they tell what is needed to preserve scholarship in the Graduate School of Education and gain respect from scholars in other fields."

◆ "Silence, you know, gives consent. Don't worry about it. I especially liked your quotes from Pascal and Dryden."

◆ "You are too acerbic. Don't you know that the best way to attract flies is with honey? Why not address the faculty in the language and style to which they are accustomed? You might get a better response."

◆ "At times you get quite personal. Aren't you afraid you might get in trouble?"

◆ "Talk about carrot and stick! First you poke, then you stroke. I like the pokes better than the strokes, but I'm sure some of your colleagues don't."

◆ "It would seem from your *Missives* that the GSE should become the Graduate School of Educational Psychology, because half the staff seem to be ed psychs. Remember, though, that at University of California, Berkeley, the Psychology Department once declined to absorb the GSE."

◆ "Glad to hear you have returned to teaching, because you will be able to put into practice the knowledge your *Missives* convey."

December 1992

81

Cool Cats and Psychologists

xperimental psychologists study animals to gain insight into human behavior. Yet they fail to realize how much of themselves they project into their "subjects." As Bertrand Russell pointed out, animals conform to the assumptions of their researchers:

They have all displayed the characteristics of their observers. Animals studied by Americans rush about frantically, with an incredible display of hustle and pep, and at last achieve the result by chance. Animals observed by Germans sit still and think and at last evolve a solution out of their inner consciousness.

Let me add that animals studied by the English know their place in the social order. Japanese animals form groups and bow deferentially. French ones are romantic and existentially self-aware.

Why do psychologists prefer rats, monkeys, and pigeons to cats? It must be because cats are unpredictable. Lewis Thomas tells us that, "The mind of a cat is an inscrutable mystery, beyond human reach, the least human of all creatures and at the same time the most intelligent."

"Some men," wrote Shakespeare, "are mad when they behold a cat." Psychologists don't mess with cats for fear they will be outwitted. The media haven't yet learned this lesson. Witness the folly of photographers, who were manipulated by President Clinton's cat Socks when they thought they were manipulating him.

"When I play with my cat," said Montaigne, "who knows whether she has more sport with me than I with her?" If psychologists can't explain cat behavior, how can they expect to explain humankind? As Isaac Newton lamented, "I can calculate the movements of the heavens but not the madness of human beings."

Psychologists have had one success, however. They have conditioned educationists to believe that educational psychologists have more to offer education than any other group of scholars. No cat would have swallowed that one. So, unless educationists acquire the sense of cats, they seem doomed to irrelevance. Their only hope is to study the behavior of cats and thus outpsych the psychologists.

Oops! I've just been corrected by scientists at the University of Tennessee. They claim that cat brains have shrunk since Cleopatra's day because cats rely on humans for food and shelter instead of taking on the wild. My reply? Sometimes smaller is better. Why should cats rely on tooth and claw when big-brained humans are easier prey?

Winter 1993

82

Golden Fleece Award #2: Sound Scholarship of Airhead Journalism?

Most writing by educationists differs from journalism only in being less clear and less informed. Below are some excerpts that deserve the Golden Fleece Award for wallowing in the obvious:

◆ In U.S. schools resources and opportunities are unequally distributed, with less going to the disadvantaged. *(News to me!)*

◆ Students with less access to facilities and materials make slower progress. *(Surprise! Surprise!!)*

◆ Schools with mainly low-income and minority students find it harder to hire and keep well-qualified teachers. *(Never thought of that!)*

◆ Low expectations lead to shallower, less demanding curricula. *(So what else is new?)*

◆ Schools enrolling mostly African-American and Latino students offer less opportunity for developing inquiry, problem-solving skills, and active learning. *(Well, waddaya know!)*

163

◆ In racially-mixed schools minority students are overrepresented in low-level classes and underrepresented in high–level ones. *(This has to be unconstitutional!)*

◆ Schools with many disadvantaged students tend to have the weakest vocational programs. *(Obviously! They have "fewer facilities.")*

◆ Because low-income and minority students score lower on tests, teachers judge them less capable of learning. *(But didn't those teachers take ed psych?)*

◆ Administrators tend to assign their less qualified teachers to low-ability classes. *(Who would have believed this?)*

◆ Students in low-track classes usually get low-level instruction and hence become low–level workers. *(Sure didn't realize that!)*

◆ Unprepared teachers are less equipped to diagnose teaching/ learning problems. *(How about unprepared professors?)*

◆ Policymakers should stress fair distribution of resources, not testing and certification. *(Come on, guys. Ask what you can do to make life fair.)*

How much real research went into these "findings"? How much hard thought? How much did it all cost? What we have here is shallow, tendentious reporting that highlights one problem to the exclusion of others. Taxpayers are fleeced, and the good name of our profession suffers yet again.

Winter 1993

83

Cant Among Curriculists

nxious to gain academic respectability, curriculum specialists refer to what they do as "philosophy of curriculum" or "curriculum theory." Yet no one has the vaguest idea what a full-blown philosophy or theory of curriculum would look like. True, philosophers like Robin Barrow and Paul Hirst have written on curriculum. But they are exceptional, and their rigor is also the exception.

Instead of genuine philosophy or mature theory, curriculists offer a mix of essayistic and social-scientistic approaches with little solid evidence to choose among them. They get top marks, however, for such verbal razzle-dazzle as "scaffolding," "fading," "cognitive apprenticeship," and "controlled floundering." No longer "learning facilitators," teachers now are, believe it or not, "information brokers."

Granted, some reflective thinking is done and some empirical investigation goes on, but it's mostly shadow-boxing, too casual for philosophy, too remote from reality for science. It also differs little from work done by educators on the job. With no mature philosophy or fully-developed theory in sight, why not call the enterprise simply "curriculum studies"?

Curriculists would like our next appointment to be a "philosopher of curriculum." This may look like a bow to philosophy and a further attempt to enhance their scholarly reputation. But any philosopher of repute would have a difficult problem getting along with colleagues so ill-trained in the structure of knowledge or the logic of subject matter. A philosopher's task is to puncture pretense and expose pedantry. To do the job properly requires considerable courage.

Why do we offer no course in the history of curricular ideas? Because there is no independent history to speak of. Curriculum is not a discipline anyhow, and if there are memorable ideas in the field, they are to be found in the history of philosophy.

Our curriculists, along with others, offer a "core" course titled "Structure and Dynamics of the Educational System." It's a grab bag of everything deemed relevant to the "delivery of education" (*sic*). Despite its good intentions, the course: (a) resembles a vaudeville show, in which one performer does his act and departs; (b) leaves to students the difficult job of integrating the contents, thus ditching the very principle of "core"; (c) boasts a bibliography that would take a decade to read; and (d) betrays its origins in a committee, being a crazy quilt of subject matter not even its authors could master.

How can teachers of teachers turn out something so unteachable? How can professional educationists so blatantly ignore the logic of subject matter and the mindset of students? How much of our limited budget disappeared in this debacle?

Winter 1993

84

No Testing
Without Equalizing?—1

f the many ideas afloat in educationist circles today the most absurd is the proposal to ban state and national tests until all schools are funded equally. According to this proposal, it's unfair to give the same tests to students who are unequally prepared to take them. So tests are to be cancelled until we have spent our way to truly equal schools .

Unequal funding may be unfair, but with governments strapped for cash, some inequality may be inevitable. Even so, how can we deny the right of some communities to spend more on their schools if they choose? If we bail out indigent schools, we may reward failure. If we reward good ones, we may spend unnecessarily. In any case, we have no real evidence that spending more money on schools in itself boosts educational achievement. Many schools do a brilliant job on shoestring budgets, even with highly diverse enrollments. They get more out of less.

Schools can't be equalized anyway, however hard we try. Even in countries that labor to level the playing field, schools vary in quality, and there is intense competition to get into the best. Again, in dirigist democracies, where spending is equalized on public schooling, some schools still outpoint others, while the private sector creates schools that are better yet.

But why the ban on tests? They may reflect unequal education but they certainly do not cause it. They simply measure performance, not the factors behind it. With test results in hand, at least we know which schools are having problems. Without tests no one is held accountable. How else will we tell where the money should go? The answer is not to ban tests but to improve them.

So students are upset by tests? Driver tests upset them too. Should we declare a moratorium on them? Without tests some students may breathe easier, but life is a series of tests anyway, so we'd better get used to them. Students should be taught how to take tests, how to handle the anxiety they arouse, how to anticipate questions. This is an educational task and teachers should be prepared to take it on.

Should teachers "teach to the test"? Yes, indeed. Tests let you know where you stand. They sharpen the mind and stiffen the resolve. But no teacher should give a test without explaining its purpose and discussing results.

Some critics want tests that are "intelligence-fair"—tests that do not discriminate against intelligences that are artistic, vocational, or inter-personal, in favor of logico-mathematical types. The fault may not lie in our tests but in the failure of schools to teach logical thinking and cultivate the one intelligence that not only aids other intelligences but enables those who possess it to reach for the heights in whatever sphere they may choose.

Winter 1993

85

No Testing
Without Equalizing?—II

ritics call for the abolition of all tests that are not passed by a "satisfactory" number of minority and underprivileged students. Alternatively, we should lower the passing grades for these students. But these measures provide one sure way to antagonize other students and breed self-hate in those who benefit from such *noblesse oblige.* If test scores differ systematically by race and class, the solution is not to screen out questions that are difficult yet fair, but to upgrade the education of the disadvantaged. In this case the scores are catalysts for change.

Even if it were shown that equalizing funding would raise achievement levels, there may be better, more justifiable ways to spend the money. There is good evidence that the cause of academic failure among the disadvantaged may not be attributed to their schooling. In fact, low–income and minority students who do badly in poor schools do not measurably improve in the good schools to which they are transferred. Achievement varies most within schools, not between them.

The evidence indeed suggests that the single most important variable affecting academic performance is the degree of parental support. Asian-American children outperform others because their families hold together and back them all the way. In this country today the motor that drives a group to success is not race or Affirmative Action, but lifestyle, including hard work.

It follows that if more money is spent, it should be to strengthen the family and firm up social services and support groups offering child care, training in parenting, and help with education. Schools should get out of the therapy business (which in their case is costly and ineffective) and get back into education.

If more money is earmarked for schools, it should be used to leverage specific reforms, such as school-based management, teacher accountability, merit pay, and tougher graduation standards. It should go to the most promising schools as well as the most deprived, to schools that are developing a special mission and character. These are the schools most likely to thrive, because they have something extra. They know, too, that the hand that helps the most is at the end of their own arm.

Visions of equal funding and a ban on tests arise from passion and ideology. They engender agitprop journalism. From scholars who are paid to think, something far better is expected: solid analysis, keen perception, balanced judgment, not a rush of blood to the head, Kozol-style. Why subsidize the output of emotion and bias, the rhetoric of race and class resentment?

UCLA no longer should tolerate professors wedded to political agendas, one-issue activists with a veneer of scholarship. It is the tragedy of schools of education that some professors, at public expense, betray the ideals of scholarship that the best of our number strive to uphold.

Winter 1993

86

At Risk in the GSE

The country is in deep trouble and this Graduate School of Education must do something to save it. That's the message behind "Risk Studies in Education," the latest expression of educationist *folie des grandeurs*.

The authors, members of our faculty, claim that their program is "highly pertinent to the mission and goals of the GSE." They don't say what the mission and goals are or what makes their program pertinent, except that kids are at risk. Fair enough, but something much more specific is needed to justify the mind-blowing parade of projects listed here.

The authors promise to identify risks that we can zap before they strike. To this end they want to study: (a) risk factors ranging from "biological insults" to "structural/environmental barriers"; (b) the causes of both resilience and vulnerability in the face of these factors; and (c) the negative outcomes of vulnerability (*e.g.*, antisocial behavior, poor peer relations, psychopathology, and academic dysfunction).

The authors have assembled a group of typical bleeding hearts to work on a program that will be "interdivisional." These academic burnouts welcome the proposal as a shot in the arm for their flagging talents. Beaten by their own life crises, they long to solve the crises of others. There's nothing more pathetic than the sight of professors who have lost their scholarly self-esteem.

Guided by this "framework" (what framework?), these specialists in agony are to study alcoholism, drug addiction, aggression, gang membership, and (ah!) school failure. This vast apparatus of research is to be trained on a gamut of problems, only one of which occurs in a school.

Soon we shall hear about the history, politics, economics, psychology, organization, and administration of risk prevention, not to exclude a curriculum and instruction in it. No mention is made of philosophy. They can't allow a bunch of eggheads to tear their plan to pieces. An unbelievable catalogue of risks is compiled and the understrappers are assigned their roles. Not until the end of the script do we hear about the educational effects of being vulnerable to risk and strategies to deal with them. Of this armada of research projects, 90 percent fall outside education.

The authors of this inane project are pretentious and foolhardy. They think that they alone are aware of the "real" problems out there. Yet when they get their comeuppance, they'll bring down others with them. The University itself may have to pay for their foolishness. If their projects lead to social missionary work, the legislature will surely intervene to place limits on what the University may do or teach.

The architects of this fiasco would serve their country better by improving their day-to-day teaching and research. The concept of risk prevention extends far beyond the bounds of educationist thinking and mocks the efforts of these do-gooders to comprehend it. The GSE, too, is at risk, for these pied pipers are luring it into academic quicksand.

Winter 1993

87

Tracking and Ability Grouping: Misinformation in Miniresearch

et against the crucial problems of education to-day, most school of education research topics are minuscule. They attract pedants out for a single topic to mine for all the publicity they can get. They promote caricatures of scholarship, compendia of footnotes, endnotes, and references, piggybacking a few pages of stultifying text.

Before me are several publications on tracking and ability grouping, each page of which could be reduced without loss to a single sentence. They are little better than student opinion pieces written for a campus newspaper without benefit of source materials. The only evidence of a professorial origin is the author affiliation.

One would think that the choice of a minitopic would enable authors to make a genuine contribution to knowledge. Not so. Some of these authors can't or don't distinguish between "tracking" and "ability grouping." *Tracking* assigns students of different ability levels to different classes or schools with different curricula. *Ability grouping* brings together students of similar ability to study the content for which they are ready. Since not all students can learn the same content at the same speed, ability groups, especially, aid the smart to accelerate, while the slow take their time. *Mixed ability grouping* assembles students of different abilities to learn the same mate-

173

rial at, alas, the same speed.

Most authors advocate mixed-ability grouping on the grounds that it promotes equality as defined by the U.S. Constitution. But these are pleas that deny the facts of biology. High flyers are asked to tutor slow learners to help them get off the ground eventually. This practice goes by the euphemism of "cooperative learning" and is "politically correct." Despite clear differences among students, it expects teachers to treat all of them "equally" yet satisfy individual needs.

These authors claim that by itself strict ability grouping has no effect on achievement. Of course it doesn't, if you give the same material to all groups. But what would be the point of that? Without more advanced material, how are the gifted to realize their potential? Without more suitable material, how do the slow improve? Ability grouping also is said to "increase inequality of achievement." Of course it does, since it accelerates the gifted. Do we want to enforce *under*achievement by feeding the same content at the same speed to all? Apparently some pedants do. (On the benefits of ability grouping see *Missive 90* .)

Camus once said, "The greatest damage to equality would be to make the unequal equal." What happens when, after being "equalized," our young people enter college or the job market and take on the competition? Handicapped by inadequate schooling, they become unequal again.

One cause of this country's decline is our preference for equality over meritocracy, except of course in athletics, where we do indeed excel.

Winter 1993

88

Hokey Ed Pyschwork: "Generative" and "Cooperative" Learning

n a recent article (*AERA Journal*, Winter 1992), two UCLA Graduate School of Education professors describe how some twelfth graders learned to "generate" ideas that altered their preconceptions and hence made it easier for them to learn new economic concepts. The students also taught this approach to one another in "cooperative learning" groups that tackled these concepts. The authors claim that the students in this experiment "increased their learning...by sizable amounts" over a control group.

Less flawed than most, this study nonetheless bears out Wittgenstein's assertion that in psychology there are "experimental methods but conceptual confusion." If educational psychologists knew more philosophy, they'd quit doing studies of this kind.

Economics is not defined. The authors cite J.S. Breneke, but the quote is just a plug for the study of the subject. Paul Samuelson is also quoted as saying, "All your life—from the cradle to grave and beyond (*sic*!)—you will run up against the brute truths of economics." Some definition! Students were also given multiple-choice questions, to which there was one "correct" answer. Yet clearly the authors were guided by a certain economic theory. If they had followed another, some correct choices would have been incorrect.

Learning is not defined, either. Most mainline psychologists have given up studying it because they can't control the crucial variables. No two people learn in the same way. And learning is more than just a psychological process, as countless philosophers have told us. Although ed psychs admit there is no comprehensive learning theory, these authors are undeterred. Perhaps they think that to learn something is to be able to answer questions about it "correctly." But answering correctly only indicates that learning of some kind has occurred; it is not equivalent to what a conception of learning would entail.

Through generative learning, we are told, students "transform the unfamiliar into the familiar by generating their own connections from that which is already understood to that which is to be learned." They "control their own learning and are responsible for being active and attentive to learning." In the experiment, generative learning was combined with "cooperative" learning, in which students form groups, whose members teach one another, swap ideas, and reach "collective judgments."

The authors "found" that generative and cooperative learning together were more "effective" than cooperative learning alone. Yet they do not say what this groupthink contributed to individual growth or what mental operations it involved.

So this study is just one more black-box account of learning, a pointless exercise in technique. Written in plodding prose, it quantifies the unquantifiable and thus contributes nothing to knowledge. This number-crunching, hard-science approach to the mind is long out of date. It's hokey. Whoever paid for this fiasco should demand a refund.

Spring 1993

89

Shove the Books!
Serve the People!
The Story of a Stanford Lad

A Stanford lad, states the *Los Angeles Times,* found something very important missing in his education—"the real world," especially "the social ills that were very, very apparent on the streets." So he took a "course in poverty" (a course?), working twelve hours a week for free in a homeless shelter. The experience was "amazing" and "stimulating."

The *Times* reporter rhapsodizes: "Public service energizes students, enhances learning, and makes better citizens.... Experts believe that more than a third of our colleges and universities have altered their curricula to mix community service with the usual lectures and term papers.... At Rutgers, for example, the number of service courses has doubled." (Not tripled—at *Rutgers*?)

We all know that students get a real buzz from experiences that are, well, extracurricular. Most of the students I took abroad on educational field trips said they "learned more" in one summer than in an entire year at a college.

But what they learned did not replace or even compete with their formal studies. Academic learning is *sui generis.* Nothing can invalidate it. If students want to do social work, they can find it on campus. There's enough poverty, alcoholism, drug abuse, rape, and racism there to absorb the time and energy of the most fervent altruist.

The drive to get universities to sanction social service projects threatens the universities' hard-won independence and their prime mission, which is to seek and disseminate substantive knowledge. Hired as scholars, professors rarely are good at solving social problems. Some can't handle their intellectual problems, so they become microspecialists in poverty, homelessness, and latchkey childhood.

Universities are in regular session an average of thirty–two weeks a year. That leaves twenty weeks for altruists to knock around the "real world." Their academic experience is *sans pareil*, unlikely to be repeated. It also is just as "real" as the world out there. Some students may have to work part-time to pay for their education, but nothing else should interfere with it. They have the rest of their lives to serve society.

The Stanford lad has overvalued "the world" because he never has really experienced it. For him, as for most students, the *rite de passage* is the move from high school to college. His education is unbroken, and college is still an extension of the known. President Clinton's proposal for national service may be a better break from formal study and a better way to serve society than any off-campus slumming. Universities should keep out of that quicksand, and professors should tend to their knitting.

Winter 1993

90

Course Proposal: "Wealth: How To Get It"

Rationale. "'Wealth," wrote Thorstein Veblen (*The Theory of the Leisure Class*), "is intrinsically honorable and confers honor on its possessor." This course is offered as a corrective to the defeatist courses on "poverty" given on some campuses. In a capitalist society, where individual money-making powers economic growth, students should learn what it takes to get out of poverty and into wealth.

Texts: Adam Smith, *Wealth of Nations*; Peter Lynch, *Beating the Street*.

Admission: Open to all UCLA students.

Enrollment: Limited only by the number of seats in Royce Hall.

Credit: Four Quarter hours.

Guest Lecturers: Business leaders and financial wizards as available (*pro bono*) .

Requirements: A deposit of $1000 to $10,000 per student, fully refundable at the end of the course. All money received, or its equivalent in securities, will be supervised by three trustees and invested by GFK.

Terms: Each student enrolled will receive a promissory note, signed by GFK, for a return of the deposit, *plus* an amount equal to the rate of inflation on that deposit over the time held. GFK will assume any losses incurred. If a profit is made exceeding the rate of inflation, GFK will retain half of it.

Note: This not a hands-on course. GFK handles the money, though students may offer advice. Moreover, at every class meeting, GFK will explain how and why he is using (or has used) the deposits to make a profit (or incur a loss).

Example: A student deposits $5,000 and receives a promissory note for repayment at the end of the course. If a profit of 10% is realized *over thirteen weeks*, and if the rate of inflation is 4% *per annum* or 1% for one-fourth of a year, the student will receive 5% (half the profit) plus 1% for inflation or $5,000 *plus* 6% ($300) for a total repayment of $5300. If a loss is incurred, the student still gets $5000 *plus* 1% for inflation for a total of $5050.

Where to get the deposit: Better keep this notice under wraps, for if Uncle Joe or Aunt Ida find out, they'll beat your door with the deposit. So will the faculty. They'll subsidize every student they can.

What's in it for GFK? The academic thrill of a lifetime. Win or lose, I demonstrate my commitment to market economics (with as much cash trickle-down to our students as the market will allow).

Who gets GFK's profits? UCLA in the form of a charitable donation!

> *Let all the profs say what they can,*
> *'Tis ready money makes the man,*
> *Commands respect where'er we go*
> *And gives a grace to all we do.*
> —William Somerville.

Spring 1993

91

Go with Ability Grouping!

n *Missive 87* I exposed some mistaken ideas about tracking, ability grouping, and mixed-ability grouping. Educationists regularly churn out "findings" on this subject that defy common sense. (One of them spent an entire book slamming schools for what she said was "structuring inequality"!). They want to equalize schooling for all by replacing tracking and ability groups with *omnium gatherum* ability groups. All students of the same age are to be herded together and fed the same content regardless of ability. This shuffle is carried out in the name of equality. **Not equal yet? We'll equalize you!**

Here's a sample of one person's thinking (and her lingo): "While some limited, flexible regrouping strategies yield positive effects on average achievement, over time the gap between high- and low-group students widens." But what's wrong with that? If the best students are allowed to realize their potential, of course they are going to pull away from the rest. That's not the problem at all. The real problem is our failure to offer less capable students material that challenges *their* potential. Then there'd be less of a gap.

Here's more: "White and Asian students are assigned to high-ability groups, over those with comparable scores, because they get help from teachers and counselors.... White and middle-class parents more often lobby schools and gain their children's admission to upper-track classes, even when

181

their past performance would not ordinarily qualify them." These statements not only belittle conscientious teachers and parents, they conceal the main cause of minority under-representation. The truth is that too few minority students apply for these programs because most feel unready for them. Apathy and humility also are responsible for their low numbers, not discrimination. Why blame parents and teachers for only doing their job?

More of the same: "It's distasteful in a democracy to make these kinds of distinctions about young kids...and it's ethically unacceptable." Distasteful? Unethical? In a people's republic with enforced equality, sure. But in a democracy that recognizes merit and rewards achievement, who's deceiving whom? Ability groups, linking content to ability, help students realize their potential. They include cross-grade classes, within-class groups, enrichment classes, and accelerated classes, with the last two producing the most "positive effects." I call that genuinely democratic.

Where mixed groups level down, ability groups give more students the chance to succeed in their own way. They provide challenging materials in a more congenial setting. Ability groups are in the American grain because they offer individual students the best chance to use their talents. They level the playing field but not the players.

In their drive to eliminate social and economic injustice, the causes of which lie outside the school and resist educational remedies, mixed-group zealots deny the right to individual achievement in the name of an egalitarianism alien to our culture. Mixed groups bore the bright, baffle the slow, and forcibly equalize all. We don't need elaborate, wasteful, blatantly ideological "studies" that deny this simple and obvious truth.

Spring 1993

92

Postmodernism 1: Wave or Ripple?

The term "postmodernism" is so protean that even Michel Foucault had to ask what it meant. Questioned whether *he* was a postmodernist, Richard Rorty once replied, if you want me to be. Postmodernism, as I see it, is a mood or sensibility that spans a broad band of our culture and welcomes diversity and fragmentation. Where modernists sought to pull order from chaos, postmodernists revel in the chaos that issues from order.

Postmodernism is a revolt against the Enlightenment, which, starting with Kant, sought rationality and progress in history, knowledge, and society. Its prophet was Nietzsche with his attack on essentialism (there is no meaning to history and no common humanity outside biology) and his reduction of morality to the resentment of the weak for the strong.

Postmodernists reject grand theories ("metanarratives"), such as Marxism (history is the record of class struggle), liberal democracy (history leads to the achievement of inalienable rights), and Freudianism (thought and action are the expression, more direct or less, of instinctual drives). Only minor theories can hope to be true. All views, writes Jean-Paul Lyotard, are worthy of respect. To criticize one view in terms of another is to "rape" and "terrorize" it.

Nothing, say postmodernists, has a nature of its own independent of human knowledge and interests. Knowledge, in turn, is simply what a particular community believes to be true at a certain time. All social constructs, says Rorty, *e.g.*, nature, human nature, selfhood, are the result of "social conditioning all the way down." If you peel off the surface, you find another layer of social conditioning. There is no essence, no independent bedrock, beneath.

Although texts seem to refer to a certain world, in fact they refer only to themselves. There is nothing outside the text, no *hors-texte* (Derrida). The meaning the author intended is irrelevant, since he or she is not there to insist on it. Texts can be deconstructed to reveal their inevitable inconsistencies, but any interpretation is always a "misinterpretation." To criticize one interpretation instead of proposing another is to "rape" it.

Postmodernists claim that broad social and political movements invariably suppress certain points of view. Groups cannot coalesce unless some are promoted over others. The only solution, says Foucault, is micropolitics, or working for specific causes, such as school reform or prisoner welfare. This is because there is no single humanity but only particular groups, such as women, children, minorities, and (more specific still) students and teachers. Groups that have been marginalized deserve to be recognized. Their needs and histories should be heard in the classroom.

Spring, 1993

93

Postmodernism II:
Late-Century Legerdemain

et past its glitzy abstractions, and postmodernism is hardly original. Stripped of its rhetoric, its theses are banal. A typical postmodernist tactic is to annihilate the most naive version of a thesis and then proclaim an opposite notion. For example, having trashed the naive view that the true meaning of a text is word-for-word identical with its author's, the postmodernists announce that there are as many meanings as there are readers.

But in reality any text has a content, and many have dates and other period features that decidedly limit the interpretations they can sustain. Kozol's *Savage Inequalitics* and Dewey's *Democracy and Education* cannot be interpreted as if they were alike. Certain things can be said of the one that cannot be said of the other. At interpretation time, texts are not simply at the disposal of their readers. They don't mean just "anything at all."

Likewise, not all interpretations are "equally good." They vary in depth, scope, and originality. Nor do all views deserve equal respect. If they did, it would take the wind out of the movement, since the postmodernists and their opponents cannot both be correct. Moreover, the postmodernist must resist any large-scale reform, involving a vision of a better system plus a critique of the current one. Both are off limits to anyone who dismisses grand views as alienating and criticism as "rape."

The Marxist and Freudian "metanarratives" may be dead, but those of Rawls, Piaget, Chomsky, and others are seeding research. In fact the yen for fragmentation presupposes the existence of comprehensive metanarratives in terms of which the *membra disjecta* can be recognized for what they are. Without some notion of a common humanity, how could different groups be singled out and celebrated? Again, how can we teach the humanities and sciences unless we assume that their guiding theories are true or at least better in some ways than their predecessors?

Micropolitics may suffice at the local level, *e.g.*, to support a teacher's strike or lobby for a magnet school. But the real obstacles to reform—entrenched bureaucracies and powerful interest groups—are going to yield only to coalitions. Rorty excluded, postmoderns bow out at this point, since they cannot help seeing coalitions and consensus as coercive rather than the outcomes of freely chosen compromise.

In the late 1950s Oxford's Elizabeth Anscombe dismissed the Continental philosophy of the day as "just gas." Though hardly fair to Heidegger and Sartre, her verdict does fit the vaporizings of Lyotard and Derrida. Rorty, too, describes his work as "conversation" of interest mostly to academic philosophers, or "notes" on some books he has read.

Having sputtered, postmodernism seems ready to peter out. Recall that Foucault closed *The Order of Things* with the prophecy that man would soon "be erased, like a face drawn in sand at the edge of the sea." Apply that to postmodernism.

Spring 1993

94

Phenomenologists on "Learning"

n *Missive* 88 I faulted a typical ed psych experiment for relying on a narrow, undefined notion of learning. Once again I invite ed psychs to take their ideas of learning from philosophers, who have studied the subject for over 2000 years. Here, for example, are the ideas of a few philosophers from a single school of 20th-century thought: phenomenology.

◆ Husserl: I learn best when I reflect on my own concepts instead of simply absorbing facts and ideas that are out there. I take these concepts from my own experience and modify them later in the light of formal knowledge.

◆ Heidegger: I learn best through creative self-expression. My role model is the authentic teacher, who is true to her own principles. Learning isn't fun. I retain most of what I have learned when in a mood of "healthy anxiety," alert, and thinking for myself. I then make what I have learned a vital part of my life.

◆ Sartre: Since I am "condemned" to be free (born to be free and can do nothing about it), I must take responsibility for what I learn. If I don't want to learn and blame someone else for this, I am in "bad faith." If I do just what the teacher asks and no more, I become dependent and lose my identity. I

187

should not expect to find learning easy. I must face and resolve conflicts of ideas.

◆ Merleau-Ponty: In the early grades especially I learn best through my senses, through perception and exploration. I also draw on "prereflective concepts," predispositons to think and act that were "sedimented" in my body in early childhood. They develop through life without changing at the core. I retain most from my study of literature and the arts. These help me to understand myself and sensitize me to people, ethics, history, and nature. They give me insight into thought and behavior.

◆ Buber: Teaching and learning are shared experiences involving communication with love and respect between teacher and students ("dialogue") and mutual empathy among students ("inclusion"). Freedom to learn is not an end in itself but an incentive to learn. I need to learn within a framework of order. I accept this order voluntarily as a result of dialogue with my teacher and inclusion with others. I do not expect my teachers to prod me into learning but to offer material when I am ready.

◆ Freire: I learn best through "consciousness raising," by finding words and expressions that fit my own perceptions of the world. For me learning is "reading my own reality and writing my own future," not simply accepting what others want me to believe. I retain most effectively those facts and ideas that enable me to transcend my upbringing and also help me to empower the "oppressed."

To anyone with eyes to see, these creative ideas of learning (and I could have chosen a hundred others) expose the theoretical poverty and practical futility of ed psych "research" on this subject.

Spring 1993

95

John Searle:
Wisdom in Academe—1

John R. Searle, professor of philosophy at the University of California, Berkeley, has made outstanding contributions to the philosophy of mind, philosophy of language, and cognitive science. Throughout his career he has been deeply concerned about higher education, from his defense of the university against radical assaults in the 1960s and 1970s to his recent criticism of the "campus left."

For Searle, much of the current debate over higher education leads nowhere. Radicals and traditionalists talk past one another without realizing it. To find out why, he analyzes the assumptions behind their stated views.

For instance, he criticizes the radicals' assumption that neither science nor philosophy refers to a world that exists independently of our ideas of it. Radicals, he says, use the same language as the rest of us. Yet this language purports to refer to public objects. Hence they contradict themselves when they use this language to claim that no such objects exist.

He also rebuts the claim that there are no objective standards of rationality. Of its very nature, he says, a claim, like an argument, presupposes such standards, since it is an act of rational persuasion, not an expression of feeling. Thus it appeals to these standards intrinsically, and anyone who claims there are no such standards *ipso facto* refutes himself.

According to Searle, university education is necessarily elitist. Since universities aim at intellectual excellence, each tries to attract and keep the best faculty and students. This aim assumes that some people are more intelligent than others, that some intellectual achievements are superior to others, and that members of a university can recognize such distinctions and act on them.

That being so, the first criterion for membership in a university is intellectual ability and, for inclusion in the curriculum, intellectual quality. It is not gender, race, class, or ethnicity, however pertinent these factors may be in other spheres. The university should seek out minority faculty and students solely to acquire talent, not to make the university more representative of the population at large.

For Searle, the university should be "intellectually" not "politically correct." Because it promotes scholarly reflection and the quest for knowledge, the university differs from lay organizations with their special interests. The university should not be a mere extension of these interests. It should preserve, pursue, and *celebrate* its own time-honored mission.

Summer 1993

96

John Searle:
Wisdom in Academe—II

 earle lays out the assumptions of "traditionalists" as follows:

- ◆ True knowledge is possible because "there is an independent reality to which our utterances correspond."

- ◆ Truth, rationality, intelligence, and intellectual achievement can be assessed by objective standards.

- ◆ Students should seek to "overcome the mediocrity, provincialism, or other limitations of whatever background they may come from."

- ◆ The chief criteria for including a text in a course are intellectual merit and historical importance.

Searle criticizes American universities for their failure to act on these assumptions, above all at the undergraduate level. "We do not have a coherent vision of what we are trying to do.... We have lost confidence in the traditional ideal of an integrated, well-balanced education...but we have not replaced it with a coherent alternative."

Searle maintains that although "we pay lip service" to the traditional ideals of equality and excellence, most professors spend little time on the undergraduate courses "that convey the Western tradition in which these ideals are exemplified." This is just one example of the "corruption" in undergraduate education.

He also accuses the university of defaulting on its primary commitment to intellectual quality, without which "we become merely trade schools or social welfare agencies." We are knuckling under to powerful interest groups (racial, ethnic, feminist, etc.) that use the university to advance their own agendas—agendas that belong in the political sphere, not the classroom, except as topics for rigorous analysis.

The university, he says, has become corrupted in yet another way. It now is seen, even by some traditionalists, as a fun place where students can choose whatever courses make them feel confident, happy, esteemed, and culturally correct. Yet a good education requires "hard thought and hard work," and it should lead to "a permanent sense of dissatisfaction." "The dirty secret of intellectual life," he writes, "is that first-rate work requires an enormous amount of effort, anxiety, and even desperation, none of which is comfortable."

Searle knows as much about higher education as any educationist and thinks more rigorously and imaginatively about it. If we were to put together his statements and those of others like him, we would know enough about the subject to retire virtually all professors of higher education and save America's universities a bundle. We would do this with confidence, because few of these professors possess Searle's profound knowledge of philosophy of mind, cognitive science, artificial intelligence, etc.—knowledge indispensable to a proper understanding of higher education today.

Summer 1993

97

For Whom Do Chicanos Speak?

hicanos are a group of activist Mexican-Americans living mainly in the Southwest. My Mexican-American colleagues inform me that using the word "Chicano" is "a political act...an act of cultural identification with one's Mexican-Spanish-Indio heritage." One who seeks to become assimilated in the Anglo-American society would not use "Chicano" (Carlota Chávez, 1977).

The Chicano movement began quietly in the late 1950s. Twenty years later it was on the front pages. How much Chicano culture *per se* has, or could have, developed in less than a generation? The cultural leaders Chicanos acclaim—writers, musicians, artists, intellectuals—are almost entirely Mexican or mainline Mexican-American.

These leaders range from radical to conservative, provincial to cosmopolitan, Christian to atheist. Having known some of them, I doubt they would have lifted a finger for the recent assault on a University that for decades has offered major courses in Mexican and other Latino histories and cultures. I myself once taught a couple of them.

The all-embracing Latino history and culture magnified by Chicanos is mostly illusion. Latinos share little more than language. Their origins and cultures are highly varied: Mexican, Cuban, Puerto Rican, Caribbean, Central and South American. Chicano hype to the contrary, most United States Latinos deny they have been discriminated against. Most would rather be called "American" than "Latino" (De La Garza, 1992). Half speak no Spanish at all. Most support bilingual education as a way to learn English faster, not to maintain cultural identity (Linda Chavez, 1992). Most follow the pattern set by previous immigrants: moving out of the barrio, intermarrying, and integrating at about the same rate (Skerry, 1993). Ninety per cent deny belonging to an ethnic group that claims to speak for them. Some radical Chicanos deny being either Latinos or Hispanics. They prefer their Indio ancestry and culture.

I have visited Mexico more times than I can count. I have published a book on the country (Columbia University Press), and I have seen, lived, and worked in more of it than most Mexicans themselves. I have a great but not uncritical affection for the people and their land. When I see their ideals betrayed by vandals, I'm appalled.

The recent Chicano onslaught on UCLA was roundly condemned not only in this country but throughout Mexico. And with good reason. UCLA is not a repressive system, still less a dictatorship. The University showed remarkable restraint in the face of the outrageous demands of a few unrepresentative Mexican-Americans and outside agitators, whose motives were more political than educational.

Chicanos now have a "Center," wrested by violence, blackmail, and threats of suicide. The mob that got it dishonored not only their own people but the land of their roots.

Summer 1993

98

"Perceptual Control Theory": A Ray of Light from Ed Psych

ongratulaitons to an ed psychologist who has seen further than his colleagues. The University of Illinois' Gary Cziko contends (*Ed Researcher,* Dec 92) that, aside from correlation studies (which exclude causes), nearly all research in ed psych takes it for granted that independent variables (usually inputs or stimuli) act on dependent variables (usually acts or responses) with no reciprocal reaction. Human subjects, usually students, are treated as the recipients of inputs or stimuli rather than as independent agents capable of controlling those stimuli.

This "one-way cause-effect model of human behavior," says Cziko, is "seriously incomplete and therefore inadequate to account for even the most mundane of purposeful behaviors." Even in a simple tracking task, like using a mouse to keep a cursor at a point on a computer screen, there is no observable independent variable. The student's actions, as he guides the mouse, depend on the position of the cursor, but that position depends equally on what the student is doing to steady the cursor. The one truly independent variable is the student's intention to keep the cursor where he believes it ought to be.

Cziko then puts forward his own model. Humans, he maintains, interpret stimuli in light of their purposes and hence "control" those stimuli. One student perceives the perturbations of the cursor in terms of his intention to keep the cursor at a point. Another interprets the words of the teacher or the text in terms of his intention to understand the subject. Thus the two variables—the teacher (or the text) and the student— interact, instead of the latter depending on the former. Cziko calls this model "Perceptual Control Theory."

Cziko shows convincingly that "input" and "output" variables interact and that mainstream ed psych has reached a dead end. His own theory is one way out of the impasse. However, I find three flaws in it:

◆ Humans do not always control their perceptions; more often they modify them. Most students taking notes at a lecture probably contribute less to their perceptions than the lecturer does.

◆ Cziko objects to the idea that an agent simply reacts to stimuli. However, it remains true that in some sense he does, since he acts in light of information he gets from them. In another sense he does not, since his intention, and not the stimulus, is the cause of his action. The crucial point that Cziko misses is that intentions control actions, not perceptions, in which case it does not matter if agents react in part to stimuli, provided their intentions control the actions they take as a result.

◆ Most seriously, Cziko still endorses quantitative ed psych. What he changes is the model behind it. Yet this does not make the endeavor any less futile. How do you place a numerical value on an intention? How do you measure the strength of an emotion? How do you quantify all the potential variables at work in teaching and learning, such as the student's mood, the argument with his parents, his boredom with the subject? The task is impossible.

Fall 1993

99

Open Letter to Dean Mitchell

'm glad to hear that a candidate has been nominated to occupy the Kneller Chair and head the Center for Philosophic Inquiry. I fear, however, that as a philosopher, he may have a problem of adjustment in the present academic climate of the Graduate School of Education.

Most of our work is no better than that of the state colleges. It hardly improves on work done by practicing teachers. Some of our inquiry doesn't touch education at all. Too many faculty are addicted to routine data shuffling they pass off as "research." Compared to specialties in Law and Medicine, ours are trivial. They contribute little more to knowledge than the daily squibs of Joyce Brothers.

True, we rank high among schools of education, but that's not surprising; their research is equally trivial. True, too, our faculty are promoted only after evaluation by all-university committees. Yet many adverse decisions have been overturned through special pleading or undue political pressure. We should seriously examine how people got onto this faculty and achieved tenure. That's one research project that would be truly worthwhile. (For example, how did we acquire so many ed psychs? Why?)

After forty years on the faculty I have to conclude that the GSE is overstaffed, underachieving, and inefficient. Our current budget buys too shoddy a product. If we kept our genuine scholars, we could get along very well with half our current faculty.

The present Divisional setup should be abolished. It's an academic and administrative fiasco. Divisions do nothing to promote education as a unified study. Division heads have neither authority nor power. Their duties are ill-defined. Faculty should make their work more useful by relating it to education as a whole rather than the specialty alone.

The GSE should stop funding research that is scientistic or peripheral to education. The processes of education can rarely by quantified, much less its ideas and ideals. As I repeatedly have shown, scientific/empirical research into such matters as teaching and learning is misguided and futile. Education is at heart a moral endeavor. It needs to be understood in terms of the ideals it realizes and their alternatives. As a study, education is a humanity. Our GSE should set an example to GSEs everywhere by building humane knowledge and drawing mostly from the humanities.

Nothing I say here reflects on your brief stewardship. I simply offer advice for the future. But if you want to create a better GSE, the road ahead will be rough. Count on me to do what I can to help.

Fall 1993

100

Valediction:
Thoughts as the Curtain Falls

nowledge, values, literature, science, the arts—these are the moral and intellectual heritage of a civilization. Some students seek this heritage themselves; most receive it from their teachers, not passively, we hope, but as active agents in their own learning. For education is the meeting of persons, in which the teacher brings knowledge to life in her own way, and the student makes knowledge his own. The encounter is subjective, in that teacher and student approach the subject matter from their own points of view. But it also is objective, since the content remains distinct from them, something in the public realm to be understood and appreciated in and for itself.

A teacher's influence on her students is immeasurable. It can last a lifetime. Students come before her when they are most receptive to new knowledge. Society's values have not yet hardened in them. To draw out the best in them is the teacher's calling, and society offers no greater reward. To present knowledge, make it clear, and relate it to the interests and abilities of different students; to encourage, inspire, admonish—these tasks require consummate skill and ceaseless devotion.

The study of this process makes education a discipline *sans pareil*. As a source of ideas and ideals, education is rivaled by history and philosophy alone. Like them, education is one of the humanities. Unlike them, it also is a practical endeavor, since its aim is to improve the process of teaching and learning and hence the human condition everywhere.

What is a discipline? It is a domain of study with a body of data, concepts, theories, and a set of techniques for pursuing and validating research. Education is all this and more. It draws on an immense range of knowledge; its scope is limitless. This vast discipline of ours, concerned with what it studies and those it serves, demands all the effort and idealism we can give it. To date the record has not been good. We must seek and gain a higher status.

One of democracy's greatest tasks is to cultivate leaders, to develop an elitism based not on race, class, gender, creed, or money, but on intelligence, imagination, and skill. Political suspicions aside, educationists are, or should be, chosen leaders; they are, or should be, members of an elite group. They must lead in the promotion of an enlightened, better-informed, and more humane society.

To win the recognition we want and deserve, we must make our study a true discipline. We must realize Whitehead's dictum that "Education requires a genius and study of its own." Until we do, our work will fall short of its potential, and our specialties will sink deeper in their tracks. It's discipline or drift. There's no third choice.

Fall 1993

About the Author

eorge F. Kneller was born in England and came to the United States at age 12. He received a B.A. degree from Clark University, an M.A. degree from the University of London, and a Ph.D. degree from Yale University. From 1929 to 1942 he taught in public and private schools, and from 1942 to 1943 served as a Senior Specialist in Education with the United States Department of State. He was an assistant professor at Yale University from 1944 to 1950, a visiting professor in American Studies at the University of London from 1950 to 1953, and a professor of education at the University of California Los Angeles from 1953 until his retirement in 1976. As a professor emeritus at UCLA he has been called back to teach philosophy of education in recent years.

Kneller is the author of a dozen books—including *The Educational Philosophy of National Socialism* (Yale University Press), *Existentialism and Education* (Wiley), *Introduction to the Philosophy of Education* (Wiley), *Educational Anthropology* (Wiley), and *Movements of Thought in Modern Education* (Macmillan)—and numerous articles. He served as a member of the board of editors of *Encyclopaedia Britannica* and as a fellow of the National Council of Learned Societies, the American Geographic Society, and the Society for the Advancement of Science.

Kneller has endowed a Chair in Philosophy of Education at UCLA and made provision for three more endowed chairs on that campus in Literature and Education, Anthropology and Education, and Internal Medicine. Plans are also underway for the establishment of a Kneller Center for Philosophic Inquiry into Education at UCLA. He has also endowed the George F. Kneller Athletic Center at Clark University and scholarships there and at Brooklyn College.

He has received honorary degrees from Sheffield University, Heidelberg University, the Institute of Political Sciences in Rome, and Clark University.

Council of Learned Societies in Education

The Council of Learned Societies in Education, a national federation of nineteen professional organizations in the foundations of education, serves the interests of faculty in such fields as the history, philosophy, sociology, and anthropology of education, policy studies in education, and comparative/international education. As an advocate for the role of the foundations in all aspects of American education, the Council of Learned Societies in Education is an affiliated member of the National Council for the Accreditation of Teacher Education and the National Association of State Directors of Teacher Education and Certification, and consults regularly with a variety of other educational organizations and institutions.

The member societies of the Council of Learned Societies in Education are:

American Educational Studies Association
Association for Philosophy of Education
Comparative and International Education Society
Florida Foundations of Education and Policy Studies Society
History of Education Society
International Society of Educational Biography
John Dewey Society
Middle Atlantic States Philosophy of Education Society

Midwest History of Education Society
Midwest Philosophy of Education Society
New York State Foundations of Education Association
Ohio Valley Philosophy of Education Society
Pennsylvania Educational Studies Association
Philosophy of Education Society
Society for Educational Reconstruction
Society of Professors of Education
Southeast Philosophy of Education Society
Southwest Philosophy of Education Society
Texas Educational Foundations Society

Past presidents of the Council of Learned Societies in Education are Christopher J. Lucas, Donald R. Warren, Young Pai, Richard Pratte, Carlton L. Bowyer, and L. Glenn Smith. The current president and vice-president/president-elect are Joseph L. DeVitis and Douglas J. Simpson. Alan H. Jones is secretary-treasurer of the Council, and the organization may be contacted through him in care of Caddo Gap Press, 3145 Geary Boulevard, Suite 275, San Francisco, California 94118.